Tales of
Whisky
and Smuggling

Tales of Whisky and Smuggling

Stuart McHardy

LOCHAR PUBLISHING • MOFFAT • SCOTLAND

© Stuart McHardy, 1991
Published by Lochar Publishing
MOFFAT DG10 9ED

British Library Cataloguing in Publication Data
McHardy, Stuart
Tales of Whisky and Smuggling.
I. Title
338.476635209411

ISBN-0-948403-86-1

Printed in Great Britain by BPCC Wheatons Ltd, Exeter

Contents

Introduction

In the hilarious film *Whisky Galore*, based on the book by Sir Compton Mackenzie, there is a sequence showing local people using a series of ingenious hiding places for whisky that has been lifted from a shipwreck. Bottles are hidden under babies, in milk churns, down drains, in a fiddle case, a clock and a host of other places. The people are seen taking great pleasure in hoodwinking the Customs and Excise officers sent over from the mainland. Based on actual fact, this film harkens back to the times when in vast areas of Scotland almost the entire population was constantly battling with the Excisemen, or gaugers, as they were known. The battles were over the almost universal activity of illicit distilling of spirits.

Fantastic ingenuity and great cunning were the order of the day as the people revelled in outwitting the government's representatives. There were also bloody battles between illicit distillers and the gaugers, resulting in some deaths. The Highlands of Scotland saw the most intense activity, but the smugglers, as the illicit distillers were called, received help and support from almost all Scots. The initial meaning of smuggling was simply the avoidance of paying duty to the government. As most of the whisky, *uisge beatha* in the Gaelic tongue, was made up in the hills in small bothies (turf huts) over peat fires, the whisky became known as peatreek. In truth the atmosphere inside these bothies was extremely smoky and often unpleasant. The spirit was also known as *poit dubh*, Gaelic for the black pot, describing the tun or vat in which the mash of fermented barley was heated before distillation (see Epilogue).

From as early as 1609 central government had attempted to restrict the manufacture of spirits in Scotland. Over the next two hundred years the government, first in Edinburgh, then in far away London, consistently tried to stop the common people having access to distilled spirits. Most of these restrictions were relatively ineffective, but they were universally resented all the same. As J. Stirton wrote in his book *Crathie and Braemar* said, ' Nothing raised the Celtic blood more intensely than any interference of the Sassenach with the old established free manufacture of his favourite liquor.'

The imposition of a threepenny a bushel duty on malt (fermented barley) in 1725 roused the anger of many Scots and the Jacobites came up with the slogan, 'No Union, no salt tax, no malt tax.' The notorious Porteous Riot in Edinburgh in 1736 had developed from resistance to excise duties. Throughout the eighteenth century the government kept trying to control distilling. They favoured the large commercial distillers of England (where gin was more popular) whose stills were generally of over 3,000 gallons while in Scotland most of the stills were of forty gallons or less. It was

6

Introduction

obviously much easier to collect revenue from the big distillers . The generally available legally distilled whisky was of poor quality. It tended to be made mainly from raw grain rather than the traditional malted barley , as much as 80% to 20%, and the subsequent spirit was too coarse for people raised on *uisge beatha* made from 100% malted barley, as are today's single malts. There was always a steady market for the high quality Scotch whisky in England.

There was a ready supply of barley in Scotland and the necessary skills were not difficult to learn. The equipment for the sma' stills was easily manufactured and soon the whole nation was awash with illicit distilling. This expansion can be clearly seen from the fact that in 1787 Dunkeld and the area north to Aviemore had one Revenue Officer, while in 1825 there were eleven Resident Officers, half-a-dozen Riding Officers or Rangers, and a varying number of Assistant Revenue Officers covering the same area. Glenlivet alone at this time is reckoned to have had over 200 stills going, and in the capital, Edinburgh it was estimated there were nearer 400. As Stirton wrote, ' In every glen the sma' stills smoked, and on every hand the warlike Gaels had warm sympathisers and were never short of customers.'

It wasn't just in the glens that this activity flourished. Stills were found in all the cities, though never in the numbers to be found in the countryside. There were regular convoys of whisky laden ponies coming into the cities. Eyewitness accounts tell of such convoys coming through the Cowcaddens in Glasgow with a piper leading them. Whole areas devoted themselves to illicit distilling - as the country was changing over to a money economy, the market of the growing cities provided a source of cash for the country distillers. At one court in Inverness in 1823, 400 people from the area of Strathglass, The Aird and Glen Urquhart were fined for whisky smuggling and related activities. That year there were over 14,000 prosecutions for smuggling-related activities throughout Scotland. And these were only the ones who were caught!

The economist Adam Smith made his feelings clear when he wrote,' The hope of evading taxes by smuggling gives frequent occasion to forfeitures and other penalties, which entirely ruin the smuggler; a person who, though no doubt highly blameable for violating the laws of his country, is frequently incapable of violating those of natural justice, and would have been, in every respect, an excellent citizen, had not the laws of his country made that a crime which nature never meant to be so.' Sentiments which most smugglers would have been happy to toast.

The smuggling began to die out after 1823 when the government again changed the law. This time they made it an offence for any landowner to let

Introduction

his land be used for making peatreek - whether he knew of it or not! Natural justice has never been involved in the formulation of Whitehall's Excise Laws. At the same time, however, the legal distilleries were relieved of the worst problems they had with Excise duties and commercially-manufactured whisky began to improve in quality. It was also a time of great social and economic change. As the horrendous clearances of Highland and Island glens spread throughout Scotland many of the people who had been active in the peatreek trade were forced into the cities or overseas.

The combination of these factors saw the gradual disappearance of widespread illicit distilling and apart from a brief upsurge in the 1880s after the abolition of the Malt Tax and the passing of the Crofter's Act the process continued until now it has (probably) disappeared. The peatreek was always sold and drunk within days of its manufacture. The quality of today's single malt whiskies is greatly enhanced by long maturation. It is unlikely that the peatreek could match them in flavour.

However the peatreek was the best of its time and at least one world-famous distillery company, Smith's of Glenlivet, was founded by a one-time smuggler. George Smith had a hard time of it for the first few years, having to make sure that his legalised still was never left unattended and he and his workers were armed with pistols at all times. Other legal distilleries set up in Scotland in the 1820s were burnt to the ground by resentful smugglers.

The tales in this book are all based on true stories of the conflict between the peatreekers and the Excise Officers charged with enforcing the Law. Stories of that conflict have survived in most areas of Scotland for the simple reason that the people throughout Scotland enjoyed the smugglers' produce and also seem to have taken a delight in cocking a snook at the Government.

Seumas Mor McDonald

In the early years of the nineteenth century the farm of *Tom-a-choachain* on the southern slopes of Ben Lawers was occupied by Seumas Mor (Big James) McDonald. Although the area is very sparsely populated nowadays even in James' time it was a relatively quiet area of the Highlands. This was to his advantage. A tall, powerfully built, handsome man James was as honest as the day is long but in standard Highland fashion this did not prevent him from being a persistent and dedicated law-breaker. Like so many of his neighbours and contemporaries the big red-headed farmer liked a 'wee drappie o it'. The idea of paying duty on whisky that they made themselves from their own barley was simply incomprehensible to many Highlanders and the more the government tried to enforce the excise laws, the more men like Big James were likely to insist on making their own. They saw no real difference between making porridge from their own oats and whisky from their barley.

James' farmhouse was set in a small wood in a secluded glen on the south of Ben Lawers and for over twenty years he took delight in outwitting the gaugers. Being a hard-working and skilful man, the whisky that he made from his sma' still was of exceptional quality and his peatreek was justifiably famous and popular in the area on the north side of Loch Tay. The quality of his *poit dubh* as the whisky was sometimes known, and his own popularity robbed the local Supervisor of Excise and his men of their best weapon against smugglers like James. No one could be found who was prepared to inform against him. Because of this James was maybe just a little on the cocky side. He remarked to a neighbour one day, " Och I don't think the gaugers can catch me, I'm in a grand place and Oscar always lets me know if there's anyone about."

" Aye, he's a fine dog," came the reply," and he's been a great help to you."

9

Tales of Whisky and Smuggling

This was a reference to the several attempts the Excisemen had made to come upon James by surprise. Each time he had had warning from his fathful collie, Oscar, who was well trained as a look-out. He needed to be, because unlike most smugglers James had his still in the adjoining wood, the combination of location and isolation allowing him to do his distilling close to home. But although he was confident, James was canny enough to realise that he must always keep on his guard.

This was especially so because of the growing resentment the gaugers felt at this Highland peasant whom they felt was cocking a snook at them. Time and again they tried to come up with plans to locate and destroy the McDonald still but James always turned out the winner. One day the local Supervisor was talking it over with his assistant.

" We've got to get James McDonald soon, he's making us a laughing stock," said the Supervisor.

"I think I've just the idea," replied his assistant, a Mr. Holton. "I've a cousin down in Ayrshire who's just joined the Excise and if we brought him in, on the quiet, with no-one being aware he was one of us, maybe he could spy on that devil McDonald and locate his damned still."

"A good idea," said the Supervisor. " We'll arrange for your cousin and another of the Ayrshire men to come up secretly. They can pretend to be gentleman walkers up from the city and spy out that still. Good, good. Now we'll have that smuggler where we want him."

So word was sent to the Excise in Ayrshire and a week or so later, a pair of young gentleman walkers were seen making their way along the north coast of Loch Tay from Killin towards Aberfeldy. The two strong and fit young men took assumed names in case anyone in the area spotted that one of them had the same name as the local gauger, Holton. They were taking no chances and they had been briefed by the Assistant at a meeting in Glasgow a few days before. All felt that the plans were well laid and it was just a matter of time before Big James McDonald was brought to book.

A day or two after coming in to the area the two gaugers Holton and Muir were on the slopes of Ben Lawers just after dawn. It was a fine bright summer's morning when they came above James' farm at *Tom-a-choachain* and they settled down behind a dyke with their telescope and their day's provisions to start spying on James. They were watching the farm when they saw James come out of the house with Oscar, his collie. Having already checked that the wind was blowing towards them, Holton and Muir were certain that they would not be sniffed out by McDonald's greatest ally, the dog. They had been well warned about the intelligent beast. The big Highlander headed up the hill on a path that would bring him past the gaugers at a distance that should keep them safe from discovery. Hiding behind the dyke they could still see their prey through the gaps between the stones. They whispered together and decided to wait until James was well past them before trying to follow him. They were quite convinced that the sma' still they were seeking was hidden somewhere on the mountain above them. They had laid their plans well, they thought, but they could not have planned for what happened next.

Oscar was scampering along ahead of his master on the slopes below when suddenly a hare started up out of the heather in front of him. Immediately the dog took off after it. The hare ran straight up the hill towards the dry stane dyke where the gaugers were hiding. Oscar fairly flew along behind it. The hare came to the dyke and with no hesitation dived through a gap between the stones and sped past the bemused gaugers. Oscar was close behind and leaped over the dyke. Down he came on the crouching gauger Muir and the pair of them rolled in the heather. Up sprang Holton as the hare disappeared to safety. Up jumped Muir. Oscar rolled to his feet, bared his teeth at the gaugers and growled. The pair ran down the side of the dyke, Oscar in pursuit. Holton and Muir clambered over the dyke. Holton tripped, Muir fell over him and Oscar leaped to the top of the dyke above the prostrate pair and growled. Sure the dog was about to savage them, the pair were relieved to hear a whistle. Oscar stood still as a smiling James McDonald came strolling through the heather. He could hardly keep a straight face. As soon as the pair of well-dressed young men had leapt up from behind the dyke James had figured it all out. He had heard there were a couple of young gentlemen on a walking holiday and here they were hiding above *Tom-a-choachain*. Well, well, well - the gaugers were after him again.

"Hello, hello, young sirs, did the dog there give you a bit of a fright," called James as he came up to the gaugers,"never you mind he won't harm you. Here, Oscar." The dog ran to his master as he reached the two young men, now clambering to their feet.

" Ah, we were - ah - just -ah- sitting for a - a rest," stammered Muir.

"Yes that's right," burst in Holton," we've been walking since before dawn and we just thought it would be - ah about - time for a rest."

" Och aye, you're the young gentlemen I heard about. Well you've had a bit of a turn so why don't you come down to the house and herself will fix you up something to eat and drink."

There was no way the gaugers could refuse and they had left their own provisions behind the dyke up the hill. A quick glance between them and both knew what the other was thinking. This would be the perfect opportunity to gain the confidence of this big cheery Highlander, who obviously had no idea who they were.

" Thank you, that's most kind of you," said Holton and the three of them set off down the hill with Oscar close on his master's heels, but turning every so often to look at the strangers.

"That dog suspects us," whispered Muir to Holton.

"Don't be stupid it's only a dumb animal, it's just not sure of strangers. We're fine," whispered Holton back to his companion.

On entering his simple but comfortable home James said to his wife, Kirsten, who was sitting by the door, " We've a pair of gentleman visitors, would you be bringing them something to eat. Och, sit you down young sirs, she'll not be long," said James as he showed the gaugers to the big table in the middle of the room. " Just sit you down and have a little rest."

At that point Mrs. McDonald looked at her husband who tipped her a wink. She then busied herself getting barley bannocks, home-made cheese, oatcakes, some cold chicken and a big jug of milk fresh from the cow and putting them on the table with plates and knives.

"Just help yourselves, gentlemen," urged James, giving Kirsten a faint nod. She turned away for a minute and came back with a big, black, round-bellied glass bottle filled to the very brim with the beautiful yellow-tinged nectar for which McDonald was so well known. The gaugers looked at each other then continued to fill their plates. They could hardly say no and both thought they were well on their way to bringing this notorious smuggler to deserved justice.

"Will you take a drop of the *uisge beatha*, gentlemen? " asked James innocently.

"We would be delighted," replied Holton, sure now that it was only a matter of time before they would have James where they wanted him.

From their very first sip the two young men realised that this was exceptionally pleasant whisky and quite unlike the standard manufactured stuff they were used to. What they did not realise was just how strong James' peatreek was. As they munched their way through the spread before them, James plied his guests liberally with the *poit dubh*. When they had finished their early lunch, their host asked the befuddled excisemen if they would like to have a look around the steading. They were delighted to accept the offer of the tour, by now feeling a close brotherhood with this fine upstanding Highlander and appreciating his hospitality. Somewhere in their minds was also the thought that now was when James was going to give himself away - perhaps the still was close by and he would show it to them, Holton thought.

As they were taken round the farm, slightly unsure of their footing but feeling far too happy to care, the young Excise officers looked into every nook and cranny of the place but of a sma' still or ankers of whisky or even bags of malt there was no sign at all. As their short tour went on James kept handing round the black bottle he had picked up as they left the house. Finally their tour was over and the two gaugers realised that to keep up the pretence of being on holiday they would have to depart. They informed their host.

"Ach well, you'll just have a *deoch-an-dorus* before you go, I insist," their host said. Although feeling vaguely disappointed Holton and Muir were delighted to have this traditional Gaelic drink-at-the-door. James fetched glasses and poured them a hearty measure each and a smaller one for himself. The gaugers tossed off their drinks and said goodbye to their very convivial host, who was delighted to see how unsteady they were on their feet as they set off down the road. You can imagine James' delight as the two happy youngsters burst into a chorus of "For He's a Jolly Good Fellow" as they staggered down the road.

It is not known what was said by the Supervisor at his office in Killin when the young men arrived there a couple of hours later but back they went to Ayrshire on the next coach, sadder and wiser than before. Within days the story was all over Tayside and the gaugers were a laughing stock.

The Supervisor decided to send for further help to rid him of the triumphant James McDonald. He had heard of an Irishman named Kelly who had had great success among the smugglers near Braemar and he sent for him to came and help rid him of this notorious smuggler whose continued distilling was making a mockery of the Excise service and the government.

The first thing Kelly heard when he got to Killin, before he even met the Supervisor was the story of how Big James McDonald had turned the tables on the spies sent in by the Excise. Being a canny and very determined man, Kelly resolved that he would bring this notorious smuggler to his long-deserved fall. On meeting the Supervisor and introducing himself he said,

" I want to know everything about this McDonald, and especially this latest bit of mischief he got up to."

As he was given the embarrassing details of the story he had already heard in the town, Kelly realised that though Big James McDonald might be getting on in years, he was no mean opponent. He laid his plans accordingly.

Having decided that McDonald's still was most probably in or around the steading at *Tom-a-chochain*, Kelly decided to mount the biggest smuggling raid ever seen in or around Tayside. He gathered a dozen gaugers from all over Perthshire and sent for a platoon of soldiers from Perth. This was going to be a very thorough search indeed. Knowing that all the natives of Lochtayside would be even keener than usual to thwart the Excisemen after James latest shenanigans, Kelly gathered his force at Lochearnhead and marched them in under cover of night to Lochtayside.

Tales of Whisky and Smuggling

It was not long after dawn when the small army arrived at *Tom-a-chochain*, hoping to find their intended victim still in bed. However as they approached the farm they saw smoke coming from the chimney and surmised McDonald was already up and about. Just as Kelly dismounted from his horse before the farmhouse the door opened and out came McDonald.

"Good morning, sir," said the powerful and grizzled Highlander, looking down at the small figure of Kelly.

"James McDonald, I am Officer Kelly of the Excise and me and my men are going to search every inch of this farm until we find the still you have been using to make whisky. You have been breaking the law of the land for far too long and I'm here to put you out of this line of business entirely," stated Kelly with as much authority as he could muster. He had never seen McDonald before and found him physically intimidating. "Right men you know what you're looking for. Get to it. You two watch him," he added pointing to the two nearest soldiers.

The search went on all day. Bayonets were poked into straw ricks, every inch of the floor of every building was inspected and the undergrowth of the surrounding wood was scoured but nothing came to light. The stream that flowed by the farmhouse was subjected to close scrutiny but nothing could be found. All that day James stood leaning on his doorpost, occasionally walking over the courtyard when a gauger thought he had found something. Not once did he say anything or move to extend the hand of hospitality. It was one thing dealing with a handful of gaugers but it deeply offended his sense of justice to be subjected to this wholesale intrusion by a small army.

At last, Kelly was forced to admit defeat. He called his troops together and sent them off towards Killin. As they left, he turned to the big, silent Highlander," Don't you be thinking that this is over, James McDonald. I have sworn to put you out of business and by God I will, or die in the attempt. "

As the small, wiry Irishman mounted his horse and headed down the road James felt a sense of foreboding. This one was different. He had been smuggling for more years than he could remember but never before had he felt threatened. He had always been sure that he could outfox any gauger in the land, but there was something about the wee Irishman that bothered him.

As James watched him ride out of sight, Kelly's mind was racing. He had a hunch that he was right, that the still was close to the steading but he had looked everywhere he could think of and had had no luck at all. Here he was on the government's business and that big Highland fool and his neighbours were all having a great laugh at his lack of success. They were all in it - that was the problem. Suddenly a thought struck him. The entire local populace was the problem, but they could also be the solution. He stuck his spurs in his horse and galloped to the nearest farm.

Reaching it he dismounted , ran to the door and knocked. The door was answered by the tenant farmer, John Robertson who asked what he wanted.

"Have you a cart? " demanded the Exciseman.

" I do. Why? " asked Robertson.

" I am on the King's business. Get your cart. I have just located the still of the notorious smuggler James McDonald and I will need you to help me carry his equipment away. Where is this cart? "

Totally dumbfounded by the news, Robertson hitched up his horse and cart and, with Kelly beside him headed off to his neighbour's farmstead. Carrying straight on past James' farmhouse Robertson stopped on the path about fifty yards from the house before what looked like all the world to be a small, heather-covered knoll. Here it was at last. Believing the Exciseman's statement that he had indeed found the still, Robertson had led him directly there.

Searching around, it took Kelly only a couple of minutes to locate the well-hidden door and enter the bothy where James McDonald had for so long made his peatreek. James himself had gone walking in the hills to try and think things through and he returned just in time to see Kelly put the last of his equipment on to Robertson's cart.

" I told you I would put you out of the business, " said Kelly as McDonald approached, " I'll see you in court. "

After almost a lifetime perfecting his skills at both making whisky and avoiding paying duty, Big James McDonald realised he had been outfoxed by the wily Irishman. After being given a hefty fine at the next court James decided to forsake smuggling and devoted his last years to simple farming. Although the odd anker of peatreek arrived at *Tom-a-chochain*, never again did James turn his hand to turning barley into the sweet nectar of the *uisge beatha*. He is said to have been the last of the smugglers along north Lochtayside and passed away in the mid nineteenth century but who can be sure that a bothy or two didn't keep sending its own brand of smoke signals to the skies above Ben Lawers long after that?

"A Good Man o'War Trick": The Story of James Gilfillan

Looking over the side of the 104-gun ship of the line H.M.S. Phoenix at the swirling waters off Portsmouth, Jamie Gilfillan let his mind drift. Forgetting the hardship, squalor and degradation of a Royal Navy sailor's life in the late eighteenth century he let his thoughts return home to the village of Killearn where just a few years earlier he had come to manhood working on the farm tenanted by his father. Home where the air was filled with birdsong and the smell of the heather.

" Dreamin' of home again, eh Jamie? " His thoughts were interrupted by the broad Cockney voice of John Hodges, the nearest thing to a friend he had on board ship.

" Aye, home, where I should never have left, " said Jamie sadly.

" No, no don't tell me about it again, please shipmate, " asked the Cockney, " I've heard it all a thousand times before. "

And in truth he had heard it all before. How Jamie had been press-ganged to serve aboard the cutter which was stationed in Loch Lomond. This boat had once been the pleasure boat Monmouth, but in 1778 on the orders of Admirals Chatham, Hood and Bayham, it had been taken into service to help in the fight against the smugglers around Loch Lomond. Once he had been pressed Jamie's obvious distaste for persecuting his friends had led to him being sent south to serve at sea. Now, after nearly two years on board Jamie's longing for home was intense. Any time he had been ashore it had been in Portsmouth under the eyes of the Marines, and his heart cried out to see his beloved mountains. Hodges knew how deeply troubled his mate was. Born into the squalor of a city hovel where poverty and disease were the norm, he could not understand Jamie's feelings, but he knew how deep they ran.

" You'll have to be careful Jamie lad. The bosun's got his eye out for you and you don't want to face the cat again," Hodges said.

"A Good Man o'War Trick": The Story of James Gilfillan

" No," Jamie quietly replied and turned to look at this wee bandy-legged Englishman from the great and mysterious city of London who had tended him with rough care after he had been flogged the year before. His care and attention had probably saved Jamie's life and both knew it. Jamie hated to think of that time, when he had been publicly whipped for little more than the fact that the bosun thought him a troublemaker in the making.

"No," he repeated, "they'll never flog me again. "

"What are you planning you mad Scotsman?"asked Hodges.

By way of reply, Jamie put his hand on his friend's shoulder and whispered, " I know what I'm doing Johnnie, so don't you bother yourself about it - and don't try to stop me."

Looking at the powerful dark 24-year-old, Hodges smiled ruefully and nodded his head. " All right, all right. I know I can't stop you, but for God's sake be careful. If they catch you they'll hang you Jamie. But if you make it and ever get to London you know where to ask for me. "

" You're a good man John Hodges and I wish you well. Thank you for all you've done for me."

"Just you be careful, Jamie my lad. " the Londoner said as he winked and turned away, his face creased with worry. He knew this fine and honest young man from the wild country away to the north had his heart set on getting back home. He also knew well enough by now that the Highlandman, as the crew called him, would die trying rather than stay on board this floating hell. Well, what would be would be.

That same evening, just as dusk was spreading across the waters and the shadows were thickening among the ships of the fleet a lone figure slipped silently over the side of the ship. Jamie knew he was set now on a road that would allow no turning back. He was deserting from the Royal Navy and the fact that he had been press-ganged in the first place would not save him from the hangman's rope if he was ever caught. But he had had enough of this charade of serving his country. His country was the Campsie Hills, Loch Lomond and the lands around Killearn, Balfron and Drymen. What did he know or care of the troubles and wars among nations. He was a farmer and had found ship-board life a torment. He took a deep breath, made sure his little money was well packed into one of the shoes he had around his neck, and pushed off from the ship. He was going home, home to the bens and the glens and the lochs, and only death would stop him.

By the time his absence was noticed, Jamie had successfully slipped by the shore patrols, met the shore-rat who had arranged to get him clothes and some food, at a high price, and was on his way. Having told his supposed benefactor that he would head straight north, Jamie went west through the dingy streets of the port, sure that soon the Marines would be on a false trail.

Tales of Whisky and Smuggling

He knew too many sailors who had ended up at the end of a rope after trusting the scum who gathered along the shores of every port to take sailors for all they could. Once he was out of the town he would sleep by day and travel at night. He was sure he could elude pursuit by taking his time and being careful. Once he was well clear of Portsmouth he could work for food. Luckily the hard bread and rancid cheese he had got with his plain, working man's clothes were no worse than the rations he had been used to. They would last him a couple of days, by which time he would be well on his way.

The next month was hard for Jamie and there were times when he almost considered giving himself up to the authorities. There were also times when the detachment of Marines looking for him came dangerously close. However by keeping clear of the highways and heading north he crept ever closer to home. When his food and the little money he had had left was finally gone he managed to eat by working for small farmers. With all the strength and vigour of his youth Jamie found little trouble getting work for food and a place to sleep. He kept away from big farms where people might ask questions. Small tenant farmers were glad of cheap labour and would ask no questions.

One morning, having slept in a hedgerow, he awoke feeling something was wrong. He opened his eyes and saw a large, middle-aged man leaning with both arms on a stick and staring at him. About to spring to his feet, Jamie froze when a deep-throated growl drew his attention to the man's companion. It was a large black bulldog and it too had its eyes fixed on Jamie.

"Fear not, stranger," said the man. " We mean thee no harm. Is it the navy or the army thou are running from? "

Astounded at the man's directness, and wondering furiously how he could have known, Jamie could only stutter, " Wh-wh-what did you say? "

"Fear not, " the man repeated, leaning down and helping Jamie to his feet.

"Thou have the look of a hunted man but I will not betray thee. Come with me and we will see about getting thee some food. Thou art hungry? " he asked, looking the young Scotsman straight in the eyes.

" Yes, yes I am," replied Jamie.

"Well, follow me then," said the stranger and turned away along the edge of the field, followed by the bulldog.

Jamie never forgot that day when a total stranger took pity on him and helped him, out of plain human goodness. Somehow he had trusted the farmer, whose name was Smith, almost right away.

After a hearty meal and with a wallet full of bread and cheese and a comforting quart bottle of ale, Farmer Smith sent Jamie on his way with clear

"A Good Man o'War Trick": The Story of James Gilfillan

directions and the name of another farmer along his way who in turn passed him on to another friend. It seemed these were people who had a religion that led them to help people like Jamie - it had something to do with being against killing, but he never really figured it out. He was just grateful for the assistance which helped him to travel quickly towards the north.

Ten days later Jamie was in the hills above Killearn. Taking great care he approached his father's croft just after dark. His welcome was tearful, his mother torn between joy at seeing him and worry about the fact he was a wanted man.

" The Marines have been here three times now, Jamie," she said holding his face in her hands, "and we're frightened they'll be coming back."

"Aye, they'll be back again alright," grunted his father. " Never mind that they kidnapped you laddie, it's not safe for you to stay here on the farm."

"I know father. I've had a bit of time for thinking on my road home and I think I will follow in your footsteps. I know just the place for a fine bothy, and I don't think the gaugers will be as hard to dodge as the Marines have been."

Both his mother and father burst into laughter, waking up his brothers and sisters, who were delighted at the return of their eldest brother.

" Right enough lad," said his mother. " That'll show the government and their flunkeys not to press a Gilfillan into persecuting honest people."

The big-bellied bottle of peatreek was brought out and late into the night father and son sat by the fire making plans and taking sips from the bottle.

With the able assistance and experience of his father and the willing help of his younger brother Andrew, Jamie soon had his bothy set up and working. The equipment for manufacturing the peatreek was set up in a cave behind a waterfall a few miles into the hills. The water would hide the smoke from the fires and the waste would run off into the burn. The burn itself supplied a pure clear supply of water and making sure that he always entered the cave over the rocks by the waterfall Jamie left no tracks. His father's experience was invaluable and soon they were making peatreek to the elder Gilfillan's recipe and even improving on it. Jamie himself had to do the most of the work as his father still had the farm to run but every so often one of his parents or his brother would arrive to give him a hand.

Soon Jamie's peatreek was finding a ready market along Loch Lomonside and as far away as Kippen and Aberfoyle. The work was hard and he had always to be careful in case of gaugers or Marines, who could return at any time but Jamie was happy. After his miserable time on board ship the free fresh air, the birdsong, the sound of the rushing burn and the beauty of the isolated glen all made him as happy a man as seemed possible. Taking time to walk to the top of Ben Lomond or casting for fish in mountain lochs he would often burst into laughter comparing his current life with the degradation and squalor of his life in the King's Navy. Though the law might brand him a deserter and a criminal he was respected by the people of the area as a hardworking and honest man. He supplied his wares to several ministers, a few officers of the local militia, including Captain Lachlan of Auchentoig, and a couple of magistrates as well, all of whom appreciated the strength and flavour of his *poit dubh*. With these contacts and his family and friends as well, Jamie was soon in a position where he would get advance warning of any detachment of Marines coming into the area. There were still the gaugers though.

About five years after his return Jamie was feeling particularly successful. He and an old friend, Ian Bryson, had been working together for over a year. Ian was of the same stamp as Jamie, a strong, brave and hard-working man of Highland ancestry. Their business was booming and they had in set up a second still to handle their orders . One day, arriving at the new bothy, Jamie was surprised to see the normally cheery Bryson sitting looking downright gloomy.

" What is wrong Ian? " Jamie asked.

" There's a new Revenue Officer been appointed at Bucklyvie and I think this one will cause us trouble, " replied his friend.

" Och, one gauger's pretty much the same as another man. None of them are keen on taking us on. " laughed Jamie in reply. " A few cracked skulls and they keep well out of the way."

" Maybe yes and maybe no, " Ian went on," but I've heard of this new one. His name's Hosie and he's a wee devil. He never gives up once he has his mind set on something."

"Ach well, maybe he's just not met his match yet," smiled Jamie. His confidence had some basis in experience. He had been able to walk through Killearn, Drymen, Aberfoyle and Kippen for the past few years without threat of arrest. However the Navy had not forgotten Jamie Gilfillan even if he was friendly with just about every man of influence on his native turf.

" I suppose you're right, " Bryson smiled back. " Whatever am I thinking of, come on let's get to work."

However Bryson was right to be worried about Officer Hosie. He had heard of the virtual impunity enjoyed by Gilfillan and Bryson and was determined to bring them to justice. By sheer application and commitment the wee Revenue Officer had managed to locate a few contemptible souls who were prepared to testify, for a government bribe, that Gilfillan was a smuggler. The bane of the smugglers' lives were those who would gladly drink their produce then line their pockets as informers for the gaugers. Hosie eventually found enough of these to think he had a case against Jamie and sent a summons for him to his father's house. Having found out all he

"A Good Man o'War Trick": The Story of James Gilfillan

could about the smuggler Hosie was sure that the man's arrogance would lead him to show up at the courthouse in Drymen, confident that he would walk away scot free. Hosie had other plans for Glfillan's future.

On the appropriate day Jamie calmly arrived at the Drymen courthouse on his own, looking as if he didn't have a care in the world. It was a fine, brisk autumn morning and he was whistling as he entered the court house.Although he looked the picture of innocence, Jamie knew well that he was in danger and was keeping his eyes open. As he walked towards the actual courtroom he caught a flash of blue in a room off the main corridor just before the room's door was closed from inside.

It was a blue he knew only too well. Knowing that Jamie had deserted from the Navy five years before Hosie had contacted the officer commanding the Navy cutter that was still stationed in Loch Lomond and a detachment of sailors had been sent to apprehend Jamie.

It was a tight corner but Jamie was a cool customer indeed. Noticing that the door that had just closed still had the key in the lock he quietly turned it and dropped it in his pocket. He then calmly strolled into the courtroom where Hosie was already present, sitting over by the window, smiling. As soon as Jamie had entered the courtroom a pair of gaugers moved to cover the door behind him.

Calmly, Jamie went and stood in the dock. Hosie stood up, proud as a peacock, ready to make his deposition. Jamie made his move. He sprang from the dock and leapt to where Hosie stood. Siezing the bottom frame of the court room window he yanked it free. With a wild Highland yell he felled the Revenue Officer and jumped from the window into the street. Amid the uproar that followed several people were laughing fit to burst. While the magistrate tried to keep a straight face as the gaugers helped the dazed Hosie to his feet a voice called out," Now that was a really good man-o-war trick. "

The voice belonged to Captain Lachlan of the local militia, a regular customer and true aficionado of Jamie's peatreek. The ensuing laughter was more than the shocked and shamefaced Hosie could bear, and he left as soon as he was able.

At the same time Jamie Gilfillan was calmly strolling through the town nodding to friends and customers as they passed. The gaugers were afraid to follow him and by the time the sailors were unlocked from the side room he was well away. Never again did the King's Navy get close to Jamie Gilfillan, whose standing in the local community had increased even further by this display of bravery and quick thinking. Poor Officer Hosie was so affronted at having become a local laughing stock that he asked for a transfer and was never seen in the area again.

Gillespie the Gauger

Of all the men who strove against the smugglers there was none more dedicated, hard-working and ultimately successful than the man known as Gillespie the Gauger. As his name tells us he was of Highland descent himself but the circumstance of his birth far from the land of his ancestors led to him being the bane of those who saw themselves as upholding the ancient tradition of the Gael by making their own whisky.

Malcolm Gillespie joined the Excise in 1799 as an "Expectant" - that is he was intended to rise to the position of Supervisor. This position found him watching over the manufacture of salt at Prestonpans in East Lothian. Salt was a valuable commodity and subject to taxation and in his two years there Gillespie was instrumental in detecting a lot of fraud. In fact he was so successful that his expectations were fulfilled and he was sent as a Revenue Officer to Collieston in Aberdeenshire. Now he could really show what he was made of.

Collieston is between Aberdeen and Peterhead and sits just north of the Sands of Forvie, a deserted area much favoured by the smugglers who brought in foreign spirits. When Gillespie arrived, it was estimated that there were 1,000 ankers or barrels of spirits being landed in the area every few weeks. Obviously the people of the north-east had a taste for good spirits no matter where they came from. Immediately Gillespie set about amassing as much information as he could about this trade. He soon found out that one of the most active of the smugglers was James Grant, a giant desperado of a man who generally went about with his two strapping sons. Intending to show his mettle right off, Gillespie, who was a powerful man himself and well versed in hand-to-hand combat, resolved to try and arrest Grant.

So he lay in ambush one night as Grant and one of his sons came from the Sands of Forvie on a cart laden with brandy. Just as they were getting near Gillespie leapt from his hiding place and roared, " Stop in the name of the King. I am Revenue Officer Gillespie and I am confiscating your contraband. "

Gillespie the Gauger

"That's what you are thinking, " Grant shouted back and leapt off the cart at Gillespie. As the two of them struggled, Grant's son grabbed two small ankers of brandy and made off. Seeing this, Gillespie tried to free himself of the father. At that point the ruffian Grant pulled a knife and attempted to stab Gillespie. Parrying the blade with the stick he carried, Gillespie became aware of his immediate danger. The look in Grant's eyes left Gillespie in no doubt that the man wanted to kill him. Furious at this turn of events, the gauger went on the attack and in seconds the notorious Grant was laid out senseless. Checking the man was really unconscious Gillespie hurried off after the son. Within minutes he found him hiding the spirits. Without hesitation Gillespie ran at his man and laid him out too. Once he had gathered the cart and put the brandy and the two securely tied Grants in it Gillespie made his way home, well satisfied with his night's work.

After this escapade all the smugglers in the area soon became aware of the prowess of Gillespie the Gauger and the incoming supply of spirits began to dwindle.

Gillespie stayed in Aberdeenshire until 1807 when his success in cutting back the contraband trade in his area gave him the opportunity to take on a fresh challenge. He was moved south to Stonehaven where the landing of contraband was as blatant as it was regular. With his usual application and careful planning he was as successful here as he had been in the north and was instrumental in confiscating thousands of gallons of contraband spirits. This was just as well because the Revenue Officers of the early nineteenth century were unpaid - they were entitled to half the money raised by selling confiscated spirits. This may seem a reasonable reward for Gillespie's activities but it really wasn't. From his half the Revenue Officer had to supply the wages of *all* the gaugers he needed as helpers, any money that was paid to informants and all the necessary arms, ammunition, uniforms etc. that his local force needed. In fact being a married man with a growing family, Malcolm Gillespie was almost constantly in debt, a fact that led to his eventual undoing.

Having proved his worth working coastal areas Malcolm Gillespie was moved again in 1812. This time he was given a large area of Deeside as his charge. His job now was to intercept the Highland smugglers coming in towards Aberdeen and wherever possible to locate and destroy their sma' stills. Although smuggling in this period was almost a national sport the conditions he now faced were different. Many of the people in coastal areas were fond of cheaper, better foreign spirits and had no real reason to help the Excisemen. In the Highland areas, however, many people saw the making of whisky as a right, granted to them by the traditions of their ancestors. Combine with this the usual Highland spirit of individuality and independence and it can be seen that Gillespie had a hard job in front of him.

Tales of Whisky and Smuggling

Again, the intrepid and resourceful gauger started out with a daring direct onslaught on his enemy. Near Skene, about twelve miles from Aberdeen, Gillespie laid an ambush for a consignment of peatreek coming in to the city from somewhere near Glenlivet. He was expecting two men but as the years had passed his caution had increased and he was carrying a pair of loaded pistols. Just as well, for when the cart came into sight it was accompanied by four well built Highlandmen armed with cudgels. They were George and John Downie, Norman McHardy and another Highlander from Strathdon. Brave as ever, Gillespie called on the cart to stop and was immediately attacked by the four men. They had no intention of losing eighty gallons of the finest peatreek to one solitary gauger! Forced to defend himself, Gillespie tried to fend them off with his own staff as he pulled out a pistol. As his assailants stood back momentarily he saw his chance. Determined not to shoot any of the Highlanders Gillespie had a clear view of the cart and shot the horse. The shot, the shouts of the Highlanders and the screaming of the horse brought a crowd of local people to the scene. Among them were the local minister and a couple of the gentry. Under their lead the local people pitched in to help the struggling Revenue Officer and the battle was soon over, with two smugglers in custody and eighty gallons of peatreek confiscated. Gillespie had had a famous victory but unfortunately this bloody episode was to set the pattern for all too many of his future encounters with the smugglers.

Aware of how lucky he had been Gillespie decided to buy and train a bulldog to help him in tight situations. Getting a suitable puppy, he called it Moss, a name that could be whispered in tight situations to alert the beast. Moss developed a range of skills to help his master, - he could snap at the heels of horses pulling carts, making them dance and spill their loads, he could sieze the beasts by the nose to the same effect or to immobilise them and he could attack the smuggler himself if directed by Gillespie.

Over the next few years Gillespie and his band of gaugers were involved in many a skirmish with smugglers who refused to be intimidated by the new Revenue Officer, and the ever-faithful Moss played an important part in several victories. There was one notorious smuggler, however, whom Gillespie could not come near. His name was Hay and, like many other smugglers, he brought his peatreek to Aberdeen from near Glenlivet, then as now a great whisky-making centre where there were rumoured to be over 400 stills working.

Eventually his chance came. He received information that Hay and his gang were due to pass by Kintore on 30th July 1816. With four other gaugers and his own servant, who was called Labban, Gillespie was watching just north-west of Kintore as dusk fell. They were just off the road. After an hour or so they heard the sound of several carts coming down the road.

Soon they were in sight. There were three carts but there were also twelve men with them, with the desperado Hay walking in front. Gillespie leapt out.

"Stop in the King's name..." He had no chance to continue as Hay charged at him, pulling out a sword. Gillespie pulled out his own sabre and parried the man's frenzied attack. Moss leapt into the fray, frightening the horses. Within seconds the scene was chaotic. Whisky barrels were rolling in the road, horses were prancing, the gaugers were fighting hand to hand against great odds. Pulling out his pistol, one of the gaugers received a cudgel blow. The blow jerked his arm and his pistol fired, lodging three shots in his groin, and he fell groaning to the road. Hay was meanwhile being forced to give ground. As one of his cronies came running to his assistance, Gillespie got in a telling blow. Down came his sabre, almost slicing Hay's cheek clean off. The force of the blow stunned the smuggler and he fell. The noise was tremendous, neighing horses, shouting men and the barking of the bulldog. As Hay fell, Gillespie was knocked over by another smuggler who threw himself at the gauger. They fell and Gillespie's chin split open as his sabre blade came down with the weight of the Highlander behind it. Managing to free his pistol he fired, catching his assailant in the shoulder. With a loud groan the smuggler rolled off Gillespie as yet another of the Glenlivet men leapt on him as he struggled to rise. As the man's hand closed over his face pressing him to the ground Gillespie bit the man's thumb. So hard was the bite that the man hauled him to his feet by the thumb trying to get away. At that point the smuggler was felled from behind by another of Gillespie's gaugers, blood streaming from his brow. There were now four smugglers and one gauger lying on the ground while the other gaugers and Labban were pointing their pistols at five more of the smugglers.

"Well done lads," panted Gillespie one eye almost closed where he had taken a blow.

"Let's get the wounded into one of these carts and find a doctor," he went on, walking over to where a horse stood shivering with terror under the watchful eye of Moss. One cart had overturned, another had spilled its cargo completely and the third seemed to be lightly laden. The escaping three smugglers had in fact made off with several small ankers of the stuff during the battle. Still, it was a fair haul with nearly a hundred gallons confiscated, though another anker had been shot through and its contents had dripped onto the road. The entire operation was a testament to Gillespie's organisation and bravery.

It was in a similar fracas after an ambush that his trusty bulldog lost its life two years later. The dog had become nearly as well known among the smugglers as its master and was shot and killed as it attacked a horse drawing a cartload of the amber nectar near Carlogie. It was claimed later

Tales of Whisky and Smuggling

that Moss was shot by accident but suspicion at the time pointed to an act of revenge - killing Gillespie the Gauger would have been a capital offence but shooting his dog was a way to make him suffer.

Sadly, from Gillespie's point of view, such famous victories in his war against the smugglers were liable to cost him more than he would eventually receive from the sale of confiscated spirits. He had to pay his gaugers, buy their arms and ammunition and pay for food and accommodation for them all when they were out chasing smugglers. The straw which broke the camel's back however was often the money that he was forced to pay out to informers. In Gillespie's own words,

Indeed captures of the greatest magnitude are attended with very great expenses; for in a country where the inhabitants are almost wholly connected with the illicit trade, it is difficult to find a person among them who can be prevailed upon to give information against his neighbour and nothing short of the Officer's Share of the Seizure can induce the informant to divulge his secret. It has principally been in this way I have involved myself in debt.

It says a great deal for his sense of dedication that Gillespie continued year after year to wage war against smugglers all over Aberdeenshire. It was also frustrating for him when smugglers were let off with light fines due to the widespread enjoyment of their product throughout all levels of society. The smugglers saw nothing disgraceful in being caught by the gaugers and in most cases they considered themselves God-fearing, honest and even respectable people. It was also not uncommon for single gaugers on the lookout for illicit stills in the glens and bens of Aberdeenshire to be caught, tied and left lying on the hillside by smugglers. With the notorious unpredictability of the weather this was a frightening experience, though there is no hard evidence of any deaths from exposure due to this practice.

Despite all of the hardships, lack of support and extreme financial insecurity Malcolm Gillespie stuck to his job. His doggedness of character would not allow him to give up on something he had started and in the end this proved his undoing.

In 1824 he was still hard at it, though his financial position was dreadful. He had been widowed a couple of years earlier and with five growing children he was constantly in debt. No doubt he always hoped that one big confiscation would see him clear and this led him to some foolhardy exploits.

In March of 1824 he received word in his office in Aberdeen that a large party of Glenlivet men would be bringing a convoy of peatreek down through Inverurie that very day. They were so confident of their strength that they were coming in broad daylight. It was a direct challenge. Without hesitation he set off for Inverurie with one gauger, sending word for others to follow. Riding furiously the two of them reached Inverurie before the convoy had arrived and after hiding their horses up a side alley just off the main road to Aberdeen. Soon they heard the sound of approaching carts. In his now time-honoured fashion, the bold Gillespie stepped out into the main road and called for the convoy to surrender in the King's name.

" Surrender! " burst out the leading smuggler. "That's a good one there Mr. Gillespie, what for would we be surrendering to two men? "

Gillespie looked and felt fear for the first time. In front of him were ten whisky-laden horse-drawn carts and at least thirty men. He had not expected this many. They were laughing and pointing at him and his sole assistant. However Gillespie the Gauger was a formidable character and he knew what to do. Praying that the rest of his gaugers were hurrying to join him he whipped out two pistols and shot the first horse dead.

"You gauger swine," shouted the man who had spoken. He raised his cudgel and ran at the Revenue Officer mouthing a stream of invective in Gaelic. Taking aim Gillespie shot him in the shoulder and then fell under the press of bodies that had surged forward from the convoy. As he fell he received a number of severe blows and just as he though his time had come he heard horses. His gaugers had arrived in the nick of time. With them was a troop of local militia who had been on an exercise. A short battle ensued between the small number of gaugers and the smugglers. The militia offered only nominal support. However, the smugglers realised that although their friends in the militia would not attack, they also would not let them beat all the gaugers into submission. So the majority of them escaped but they left a few of their number wounded or unconscious and half a dozen carts of peatreek.

When the bloody Gillespie was hauled to his feet he still managed to call out, " Well done lads, another famous victory. We'll all do well out of this one," before being helped to a nearby inn where a doctor was sent for. In this skirmish he had received two bad wounds bringing the number of injuries he received in his career to forty-two. His luck had held and yet again he had proved triumphant.

His luck was running out however. Since the change in the licensing laws of 1823 the quality of factory-made spirits had greatly improved and the demand for peatreek was beginning to taper off. Changes in the law affecting the land on which whisky was made also made it difficult for landlords and other gentry to turn a blind eye. No longer could Gillespie hope to stay out of debt by confiscating more and more peatreek. The Inverurie convoy was one of the last of its size and the production of peatreek itself was beginning to tail off, though there was a great deal of activity for a few years more. Yet Gillespie was still deeply in debt.

Having spent almost thirty years chasing the smugglers on behalf of the government he was poorer than when he had started. Concern for the welfare of his five children now led Malcolm Gillespie into the tragic mistake of his life. In order to boost his income he began to falsify returns of whisky destroyed and confiscated.

It was only a matter of time before he was arrested and jailed in Aberdeen. Forgery was a capital crime and there was no doubt that Gillespie the Gauger was guilty. The verdict was a foregone conclusion. While in jail awaiting trial and sentence the redoubtable and respected Revenue Officer wrote a booklet entitled *The Memorial and Case of Malcolm Gillespie.* The booklet was an attempt to 'put the record straight' and also was something of a plea for clemency. The plea failed and on 16th December 1827 Malcolm Gillespie was hanged in Aberdeen.

The booklet he wrote contains lists of all the spirits confiscated or destroyed by the author in his career as a gauger. The overall total is well in excess of 25,000 gallons. It is a particularly sad reflection on the state of the licensing laws of the country in the early eighteenth century that not only did the majority of the populace flout the laws but the most successful of all the Revenue men went to his death because he was forced to steal to look after his family.

The Lang Auger

The people of the area of Strathglass, Urquhart and the Aird to the west and north of Loch Lomond were as dedicated to the manufacture of the peatreek as any in the Highlands. At *one* Justice of the Peace Court in Inverness in 1823 no fewer than 400 people from these districts were fined for smuggling. As not everybody involved with the peatreek was caught it is clear that virtually everybody in the population must have at least known someone who was involved. As the author of *An Angus Parish in the Nineteenth Century* wrote " In every glen the sma' stills smoked and on every hand the turbulent Gaels had the warmest sympathisers and were never short of customers." That was in an area far to the south so it is easy to imagine just how widespread and well supported illicit distilling was in Inverness-shire.

In the early years of the nineteenth century the village of Abriachan overlooking Loch Ness was a particularly busy place for smuggling. The local people were constantly on the lookout for the gaugers. One sma' still, run by Donald and Alistair was being operated in a cave near the shore of Loch Ness. One day the gaugers found the cave. Luckily they were seen by a couple of young lads who had been out fishing. On seeing the gaugers they ran for Abriachan. Arriving at the village they ran to Donald's house.

Responding to the loud hammering on his front door Donald appeared and saw the young lads," Whatever is the matter, boys?" he asked.

Winded by their exertions the laddies managed to stammer out that the gaugers were at the cave.

"What? They have found my cave have they? Right we'll soon sort them," replied Donald, grimly.

First he ran for his partner Alistair and told him the news. They then split up and went round every house in the village. Soon they had a sizeable crowd gathered and they set off for the hilltop above the cave. It had taken less than ten minutes to gather the sympathetic crowd.

Tales of Whisky and Smuggling

The gaugers were just beginning to carry the dismantled still out of the cave when stones began to land among them. One man was hit on the shoulder by a small boulder and fell to the ground screaming.

"Look out," cried the Officer. " Quick, get up the hill after those damned smugglers! You two stay behind," he shouted to his men. The smugglers were raining down stones from the hill above. Try as they might, the gaugers kept being driven back by the hail of stones . On the hilltop the men and women of Abriachan were jeering at the besieged government men. The situation appeared hopeless, but the officer was not about to give up his find. He had also managed to locate another two stills in a nearby birch-wood, where they had tethered their horses and left their cart, and he was set on retaining all three of them.

"Thomson," he said to one of his men, " make a run for the horses and fetch troops from Inverness. We'll stay here and watch the stills. Quick, be off with you."

Even on horseback it took over an hour for the troops to arrive. In the meantime the gaugers kept trying to get up the hill to the smugglers but were driven back each time. Still they kept trying. Eventually the Officer's patience was rewarded. Thomson and a detachment of armed dragoons came into view along the Lochside road. At once the gaugers gave a cheer and as the dragoons drew close they came out of the cave and started up the hill towards the smugglers. Down came another hail of stones. Back they ran. The Dragoons officer came up to the gaugers and the stones stopped falling.

" Right ," said the Revenue Officer," clear those people from the top of the hill. In fact arrest them all," he demanded, " they have injured four of my men. "

"Just a minute. " replied the officer, a cornet called Browne who had developed a taste for peatreek since being posted to Inverness," What is the charge to be against these people?"

"What?" spluttered the exciseman, " They have assaulted officials of the government. They are all smugglers, as you well know. " He stopped a moment then said, "They are guilty of rioting too. Now do your duty man."

Reluctantly the dragoon officer called his men forward and told them to clear the hilltop. Deliberately and slowly the dragoons dismounted, took their firearms and began to walk up the side of the hill. The Revenue Officer looked grimly on then told his men, " Right gather up the equipment and we'll go get the other two."

On the hilltop, the villagers of Abriachan had no intention of tangling with the troops especially as they were usually such good customers. When Donald said, "Let's go back home," they all realised sadly that this time the gaugers had a victory. Of Alistair though there was no sign.

As the gaugers returned to the birch wood with the still from the cave and three of them began to load the equipment the others set off to get the other sma' stills. But there was not a sign of them to be found. While the Officer had thought he was being clever by sending for the troops, Donald and Alistair had used the time to organise matters to their own benefit. So a great victory for the gaugers wasn't quite so great after all.

However not every encounter between gaugers and smugglers resulted in minor injuries. In Strathglass, a few miles west of Abriachan, about the same time, a real tragedy happened. A quantity of fresh-made peatreek was being stored in a barn near Glassburn and somehow the gaugers got to hear of it. It was waiting to be transported to Inverness, where there was a great demand, and the gaugers moved swiftly. However their arrival in Strathglass just before dark was spotted and by the time they arrived the barn was manned by smugglers armed with cudgels and ready to defend their merchandise. One of the gaugers, relatively new to the job came round the back of the building. A string of Gaelic gave the location of a smuggler peering through the gaps in the wicker-work door of the barn. Almost without thinking the gauger stepped forward and thrust his cutlass through the wicker-work and pierced the man in the chest. With a groan the Highlander fell. The gauger stepped back. The officer ran up.

"What have you done," he demanded. Looking at the blood dripping from the man's sword he needed no answer. " My God, you've killed one of them. Away men, away, quickly, make for the horses " he cried, running for the horses a few hundred yards away. They had left them there to approach the barn on foot, hoping to have the advantage of surprise. Getting into a fight and ending up with the whisky was all very well - a few broken skulls or limbs was acceptable - but killing one of the smugglers was something else again. The Strathglass men would neither forgive nor forget that.

As the gaugers ran for their horses the smugglers came out of the barn and gave chase. Running down the hill in the gathering dusk the gauger at the rear stumbled and fell. He had no time to get back up before the smugglers arrived. Whether they could see him in the dark or not the smugglers all trampled over the gauger and pursued his colleagues, who got to their horses and rode furiously away. On returning, the smugglers found the trampled gauger still lying on the path. He was unconscious and obviously badly injured. The smugglers picked him up and carried him a couple of miles to the Bogroy Inn where he was put to bed. Sadly however he had sustained internal injuries and two days later he died. The smuggler who had been stabbed was on his feet within ten days. Because of the dark, the gaugers could not tell who had been in the barn. It was the inexperience of one of them that had led to the tragedy, and the matter was quietly dropped. No one was prosecuted over the death.

The Bogroy Inn also features in a story that has other versions all over Scotland.

A bunch of young men were running a still on the slopes of Carn Mor. One of them, Ewan McLeod, was involved with a young lass called Mairi who worked as a maid in the Bogroy Inn. Ewan spent almost as much time at the inn as he did at the still and had to put up with a lot of banter from his fellow distillers.

"Och aye Ewan, you'd be better off being caught by the gaugers. She's a lovely girl Mairi but she'll have you tied hand and feet before you can blink," was a typical comment from his friend Hamish, with whom he'd built the bothy. However Ewan was not to be put off by such silliness. He knew Mairi was just the girl for him and snorted, "If you find anyone at all who'd put up with your coarse ways Hamish McDonald, pigs will fly. Come on we've to leave this anker for the minister at the usual place." So they set off taking turns carrying the anker and hid it in a hollow tree by the road not far from the Bogroy Inn itself.

When they had hidden the anker Ewan was about to head to the inn when Hamish put his hand on his arm and pulled him round.

" Come on now Ewan we've a batch of malt to soak. Once that's done you'll have time to visit a while with your Mairi," he said. Ewan agreed with a bad grace and they set off back up the hill.

They had put the malt in the burn by their bothy and were back tending the worm as dusk began to fall when a figure came in sight walking briskly up the hill toward them.

"It's Mairi," said Ewan ," I wonder what's up." He ran through the heather to greet his sweetheart.

"Mairi, it's grand to see you but..." he started.

"Never mind that Ewan," panted Mairi. " Three gaugers have come to the inn and they have got the ministers' anker with them."

" How did that happen?" demanded Hamish who had just run up.

"I don't know," replied Mairi catching her breath, " they just came in with the anker and said they wanted a room."

"What for would they want a room? " asked a puzzled Hamish.

"They said it was too late to take the anker back to Inverness tonight so they'll stay overnight at the inn," Mairi told him.

"Right," Ewan had a determined look in his eye. " Let's go down to the inn."

"Ewan, Ewan, we can't have any trouble at the inn, please," pleaded Mairi, knowing her young man to be fearless and quick to anger.

"No, no, no," said Ewan pensively, " I think I maybe have a plan. Hamish you stay here with the still. I'll get Iain and Jamie to give me a hand on the way." A little while later, Ewan and Mairi arrived at the Bogroy Inn with Jamie and Iain. The gaugers were nowhere to be seen. A quick enquiry ascertained that two of them were in the room directly above the bar room with the whisky while the third had gone off to Inverness. On hearing the news Ewan smiled. " Mairi, I think you should go and see if the gentlemen upstairs are in need of any refreshment."

A few minutes later Mairi came back down and informed the landlord that they wanted some food and two tankards of beer.

" Well then, where's the anker in the room?," Ewan asked Mairi.

" It's a few feet in front of the door but one of them is sitting on it. I heard him tell the other he'll sleep sitting on it so none of you damned smugglers will sneak it away," she told him.

" Och well," smiled Ewan," maybe we will let him have the anker. Now when you go back up, pace out how far from the door the man is sitting on our hard-earned peatreek."

" I will, but why?" asked a puzzled Mairi. Ewan merely winked in answer.

As she collected the food and drink for the revenue men she saw Ewan whispering with Iain and Jamie who both left immediately. She looked over at Ewan who merely smiled and nodded.

So Mairi went back upstairs and carefully walked right up to the gauger sitting on the barrel.

"Here you are sir," she said handing him the plates and turning to hand his partner the tankards. Holding the two plates the first gauger smiled at her and said, " You're a pretty lass then. Would you like to share a drink with two of His Majesty's Revenue Officers?" he asked.

"Enough Thomson," interjected the other gauger. " We're here on business and she's probably in with the damned smugglers. You've done your work girl, now go." As she left she heard the door being bolted behind her.

Returning downstairs she saw Ewan in conversation with the landlord. Seeing her he turned and asked, " Well, my love, can you pace out the distance for me? Start at the door there. It's directly under the one above"

Mystified, she did as she was told and moved away from the spot she had stood in as Ewan took her place, a beaming smile on his ruddy face.

"Right," he said, "would you bring me a stool now. We've a bit of a wait I think."

Placing the stool directly below where the gauger was in the room above, Ewan sat down and had a glass of peatreek as he waited for his friends' return. Soon Jamie was back with an empty anker the same size as the one above and a long thick piece of straw. Mairi looked quizzically at Ewan who only smiled and sipped his glass. A wee while after that, Iain returned carrying an auger or drill, about three feet long. All three implements were placed behind the bar as the three young men sat and quietly chatted, occasionally sipping at their whisky.

Just after midnight Ewan whispered to Mairi, " Go on up and have a listen at the door, my love."

She did as she was asked then returned and whispered , " It sounds as if they are sleeping."

"Good, good," said Ewan calmly and went to get the implements. After carefully oiling the bit of the long auger and positioning his friends just right he climbed on the stool. Looking up through a tiny chink in the floorboards he gave a satisfied grunt and raised the auger. Carefully, he inserted the point of the bit in the ceiling and began to turn the auger. The iron bit into the wood and shavings began to fall. After a couple of minutes of careful steady drilling he asked, " Are you ready? ". His friends replied that they were. Two more turns and a flow of golden liquid ran down the auger. Quick as a flash, Ewan removed the drill and leapt from the stool. Jamie took his place immediately and inserted the straw in the hole. Behind him Iain held the whisky barrel up to the bottom end of the straw. Down through the straw the amber liquid poured. Within minutes the exchange was completed and the barrel was bunged.

"Right," said Ewan, "just take it straight to the minister Jamie, he's waited long enough."

"Well done, Ewan," said the landlord, "Well done indeed, have a dram on me."

"All right, just the one," replied a beaming Jamie as the locals who'd sat quietly with him gave him their whispered congratulations.

In the morning the gauger got up from the barrel he'd been sitting on. As he did so the anker fell over and rolled across the floor. The two gaugers looked at each other and left as quickly as possible trying to ignore the small smiling crowd that had gathered inside and outside the Inn.

"I hope you had a good-night's sleep," a voice called out.

"Aye, they're heavy sleepers the gaugers, "came another.

" It wasn't from under your nose it was taken, now was it?" laughed a third voice.

The gaugers left with the jeers and laughter of the locals ringing in their ears and it was a long time before any of that particular trio showed his face anywhere near the Bogroy Inn.

The Battle of Corriemuckloch

In the beautiful hills between Crieff and Amulree just north of the Sma' Glen, lies Corriemuckloch. Here in the early years of the nineteenth century a famous confrontation took place between smugglers and a party of the Scots Grey Guards. It was in fact a pitched battle and attained such celebrity that a local ballad was written about it, which was popular in the Crieff district for a long time.

At the time, the whole area surrounding Breadalbane and Strathtay was notorious for the amount of smuggling that was being carried out. As in many other areas the relationship between the smugglers and the gaugers varied from outright hostility to mutual tolerance. An example of the latter was the story of Willie McGregor from Lochlane, near Crieff, a smuggler who had his still over by Callander. He was a cousin of Donald McGregor, of whom we will hear more later. One evening, Willie was driving his cart towards Crieff when he spotted a weel-kent figure on the road ahead. It was the local Supervisor of the Excise Mr. Graham. There was no way to avoid him and Willie had a good load of peatreek on the cart. So as he approached the chief gauger he brought his horse to a halt.

" Good evening, Mr. Graham," Willie sang out.

" That's as may be, McGregor. I think I'll have a look in that cart of yours," replied the Exciseman.

As he dismounted and came alongside the cart Willie's mind was racing. How could he avoid losing his load? Never mind if he was imprisoned overnight or fined the next day, he didn't want to lose his peatreek. He had worked long and hard and had customers waiting. Customers who knew the risks of the smuggling trade but would be awful disappointed if they didn't get the whisky they had ordered. Suddenly he had it.

" Aye it's a fine night Mr. Graham. How is Mistress Graham, I have a wee bit bundle here to deliver to her. She's at home the now is she?" he innocently asked.

35

Tales of Whisky and Smuggling

Graham stepped back from the cart as if he had been stung.

"What's that you say? Never mind, never mind, just you carry on on your way," blustered the gauger. His wife had never told him exactly where she got the whisky he enjoyed at home, though he knew well enough it was local stuff. Like most people he preferred the "real stuff" and was perfectly aware of the double standards this showed. However, he was generally conscientious in his duties and felt he could let just this one smuggler go on his way unmolested.

As he rode on, Willie congratulated himself on his swift thinking. Of course he had no "wee bit bundle" for Mrs Graham, but he had got his load past the Exciseman. After delivering his load Willie decided to play safe and go home the other way, round by Comrie. Whom should he meet on the road but Graham again.

It was well known that Supervisor Graham liked the odd glass himself and by the look on his face he had had a few since they had met earlier in the day. Nothing would do but that the gauger buy Willie a drink in the inn near Quoig. With many a wink and nudge, Willie and the gauger had a couple of glasses. Then, pleading business elsewhere, WIllie managed to get away from Graham. He appreciated that it was handy having a friend among the gaugers but he was also aware of what would happen when Graham found out he had been fooled. Heading home to Lochlane he found his cousin Donald waiting for him. On hearing the story of what had happened, Donald knew just what to do.

"It's still early, Willie. Graham will be a while in the inn yet I think, so, just you get another barrel and drop it off with his wife - and don't ask her for payment, she'll keep quiet too I'm sure, " he told his cousin. So yet again Willie set off to Crieff, managing to avoid the gauger this time.

Donald's advice had served his cousin well. However, it was not too long after this that Donald himself was involved in the famous Battle of Corriemuckloch. He had his still up in the higher reaches of Glenquaich through which ran the road from Kenmore to Amulree. It was his usual habit to team up with other tenders of the peatreek flame to transport their wares to Crieff and sometimes beyond. These regular convoys could have over thirty whisky-laden ponies and upwards of a dozen hardy smugglers. Skirmishes with the Excise were frequent but pitched battles were rare - big convoys always had scouts out in advance and, with information from the whisky-loving local people they, could generally get through safely. One or two gaugers who came across such a convoy would inevitably send for help. When such help arrived it was usually to find that the smugglers had got clean away. It was a frustrating experience for the gaugers. However their traditional weapon of bribery brought them occasional cause for celebration.

One such occasion took place when Donald McGregor and his friends in

The Battle of Corriemuckloch

Glenquaich had prepared a considerable convoy to go to Crieff. It was December and the people of the nearby town were awaiting the supplies of the finest peatreek they could find to celebrate the forthcoming Hogmanay. The smugglers had plenty orders and had been working hard to make enough peatreek to satisfy their customers. However one of Donald's friends had had a quarrel with one of his neighbours. The quarrel had come to blows and the smuggler had turned out victorious. The loser decided he would have his revenge. As the smugglers generally trusted their neighbours it was easy for him to find out when the next convoy would be heading south. The date set was the 21st December and he duly informed the gaugers the day before when he had cause to go in to Crieff. He went and personally informed the Supervisor, Mr Graham. At this time, a small detachment of Scots Greys was billeted at Auchterarder and Mr. Graham siezed his chance. He sent a messenger to the dragoon officer and asked for his help. The young cornet was bored and the opportunity for some action delighted him. Accordingly the Scots Greys arrived in Crieff that evening under cover of darkness as Graham had suggested. He saw no reason to take chances and was well aware that for every spy he could find, the smugglers could rely on dozens.

The following day the combined force set off towards the Sma' Glen. Graham knew the smugglers would have to come this way and was determined to stop them. He knew they would be stopping at Amulree to meet others from Strathbraan and had been told they would be setting off just before dark. He had laid his plans accordingly and passed through the Sma' Glen not long before darkness fell. On the shortest day of the year darkness would come just after four o'clock and Graham knew that this was when the smugglers would start for Crieff. However, the smugglers had gathered at Amulree just after one o'clock and Donald McGregor had sent out a couple of young lads to spy out the road ahead. He wasn't expecting trouble but there was no point in taking unnecessary chances. Just as they were setting out for Crieff the two young scouts came running up the road.

"Donald, Donald, we heard a whole load of horses coming up through the glen," one of them called.

"Right lads," cried the quick-thinking Donald. " Half of you get the ankers off the ponies and hide them in the moss. The rest of you come with me." As the smugglers sprang to remove the barrels and hide them in the boggy ground to the west of the road Donald quickly gave out instructions to his remaining companions. All were young, strong men armed with oak cudgels and most had proven their mettle in previous encounters with the representatives of the government.

" Now here's what we'll do. They'll be here soon so keep quiet 'till they're almost on us then start screaming and yelling. That way we'll maybe frighten their horses into throwing a few of the pests," he told them. " You all know what to do and once we've got them on the run we can come back for the barrels."

The smugglers formed a line across the road with a dyke on the left and the bog to the right. By now they could hear the approaching horses. It was obviously a large party that was coming carefully along the road in the dark, but the plans were laid and no one would quit now. The gaugers and dragoons came up the glen. Before they knew it there was a great shout and the smugglers ran at them. The dragoons had no time to draw their weapons. Several horses reared in panic. Others turned into the boggy moss at the road side. Several of the government party were thrown and the smugglers were among them. Wielding their cudgels and sticks, the smugglers began to drive the dragoons and gaugers back.

"Regroup, regroup! " shouted the young cornet as his troops fell back. Several had managed to draw their swords and put up a good fight while their companions who had been thrown retreated down the road. Again the officer shouted an order and those of the soldiers still on horseback drew their carbines and fired over the smugglers' heads. The light of the carbine flashes showed what seemed to be a host of smugglers. Several of the horses were floundering in the morass of the bog and their riders had a difficult job controlling them. The rifle fire made the smugglers stop momentarily, then they pressed forward again. The soldiers just had time to regroup before the fresh onslaught came. In the dark there was little advantage being on horseback and some of the dragoons began to fight on foot. Their enemies however were on home ground. Men would jump over the dyke at one point only to appear behind the troops and gaugers moments later. They also seemed to know just where there was firm ground in the moss. The hand-to hand fighting was furious, sword against cudgel. All the time Supervisor Graham was shouting," Lay down your arms in the King's name. I am the Supervisor of Excise and you are all under arrest."

No-one paid him any attention as the fight raged on. Soon the smugglers were joined by the rest of their party, who had hidden the barrels they were determined to protect among the moss nearby.

Slowly, the troops who had formed a line between the gaugers and the smugglers began to fall back. Inch by inch they retreated. Their officer might be keen on helping the Excise but the ordinary soldiers had no real heart for this work. They defended themselves stoutly but made no real effort to take the attack to the enemy. Most of them liked a drop themselves and were none too keen to help the gaugers at any time. It was commonly believed that most dragoons had developed a great thirst in tackling Napoleon's cavalry at Waterloo, and that they had never got over it. In fact many of them took advantage of their searches to hob-nob with the smugglers and partake of as much good whisky as was available. Some were even actively involved in assisting smugglers. Though the smugglers were pressing hard, they had no real wish to do the soldiers harm . Their enemies were the gaugers. Mainly they were trying to protect their goods, the glorious amber nectar they had worked so hard to produce. Suddenly the smugglers pressed harder. A trooper was struck over the head as he bent down to parry another swinging cudgel. He fell from the saddle, stunned. His startled horse galloped through the smugglers who jumped out of its way. Seeing the soldier lying on the ground the nearest smugglers drew back. Suddenly all of the Highlanders who only moments before had been fighting so fiercely, disappeared into the night. The soldiers gathered round their fallen comrade. Luckily he was still breathing, but his head was covered with blood pouring from a gash in his head. In the darkness now there was no sign of the smugglers.

"Right men," cried the cornet, " Let's get him under cover. We'll take him to the inn at Amulree."

"But what about these damned smugglers and the whisky?" demanded the Supervisor.

"My first responsibility is to my men,' the Cornet frostily replied. " Come on men."

So, carrying the injured soldier they headed for the inn at Amulree, carbines at the ready. There was still no sign of the smugglers. They had retreated when the soldier fell. Those nearest thought he was dead. However, Donald and a couple of others had stayed close by in the peat moss and heard the officer say he was alive. So they let the troop head on to Amulree with the injured soldier.

"Let them go on through," Donald whispered to the man nearest. " We've saved our ankers, that's enough." Quickly the message was passed among the smugglers and all stayed out of sight as the Scots Greys came through. With one of their number injured they would not be so loath to fight as before. The gaugers held a quick, whispered conference, looking constantly over their shoulders. Without the soldiers they were greatly outnumbered and experience told them the smugglers would not be far off. Quickly, they mounted their horses and headed back south, with faint sounds of jeering and laughter in the darkness behind them.

The following morning, the injured soldier's horse was found grazing quietly, by the roadside five miles down the road to Dunkeld. Over the next few weeks the smugglers retrieved the hastily hidden barrels of peatreek from the moss, keeping a weather-eye open for the gaugers who they knew would be watching out for just such an eventuality. However, not all of the ankers were found - some had been hidden too well!

The news of the battle spread round the locality and soon a song was written and being sung about what was regarded as a victory over the gaugers and the government itself. The song shows clearly that the smugglers were seen as the heroes and the government's revenue men as the villains.

The Battle of Corriemuckloch

December, on the twenty-first,
A party of the Scottish Greys
Came up our lofty mountains steep
To try and Highland whisky seize,
With sword and pistol by their side,
They thought to make a bold attack
And a' they wanted was to seize
Poor Donald wi' his smuggled drap.

Chorus
Dirim dye a dow a dee,
Dirim dye a dow a daddie,
Dirim dye a dow a dee,
Poor Donald wi' his smuggled drap.

The gauger loon drew up his men,
And soon poor Donald did surround;
He said, " Your whisky I must seize
By virtue of the British Crown."
"Hip, hip!" said Donald, "not so fast,
" The wee bit drappie's a' our ain;
We care not for you, nor your horse,
Nor yet your muckle bearded men."

The Battle of Corriemuckloch

The Highland chields were soon drawn up,
With Donald chief to give command;
But a' the arms poor Donald had
Was a good oak stick in ilka hand.
Brave Donald smartly ranged his men
Where a stane dyke was at their back;
And when their sticks to prunock went
Wi' stanes they made a bold attack!

But ere the action's brunt was o'er
A horseman lay upon the plain,
And Sandy then to Donald said,
" We've killed ane o' the bearded men."
But up he got and ran awa',
And east to Amulree he flew,
And left the rest to do their best,
As they had done at Waterloo.

When Donald and the lads struck fast,
The beardies had to quit the field;
The gauger's men were thumpit weel
Ere driven back and forced to yield.
" If e'er ye come this gate again
Ye filthy, ugly gauger loon
If e'er ye come through Almond's glen,
Ye'll ne'er see Auchterarder toun."

When the battle's din was o'er,
And not a horseman to be seen,
Brave Donald to his men did say,
" Come, sit ye doun upon the green.
And noo, my lads, ye just shall taste
A drappie o' the thing we hae.
"My troth," quo' Donald, " they did get
A filthy hurry doun the brae."

drap - drop; *loon* - fellow; *ain* - own; *muckle* - large; *chield* -young man; *ilka* -
each; *stane* -stone; *dyke* - wall; *prunock* - pounding; *awa'* - away; *thumpit* -
thumped; *weel* - well; *gate* - way; *brae* - hill.

Tales of Whisky and Smuggling

The injured soldier soon recovered, and he and his comrades harboured no thoughts of revenge against the Glenalmond smugglers. The gaugers were of course mortified and had to put up with hearing the "Battle of Corriemuckloch" sung or whistled as they went about their day-to-day lives. Donald and the rest of the Glenalmond men carried on making peatreek and sending it south and for a few months at least had a clear route through the Sma' Glen as the gaugers kept out of their way.

Up Glenisla

Running north and west from the great valley of Strathmore into the Grampian mountains, Glenisla is steeped in stories of the past. Here battles were fought between clans and against raiding caterans throughout many centuries. It was here that the famous archer Cam Ruadh developed his skills and entered legend after the Battle of Cairnwell in the late seventeenth century. Here too the people retained that individuality of spirit and independence of thought which so characterised the Scottish Highlands. It is therefore hardly surprising that Glenisla was the scene of a great deal of whisky smuggling in the late eighteenth and early nineteenth centuries. The surrounding hills provided numerous hidden locations for bothies where the gaugers would never find them. The Glenisla peatreek was well-known and appreciated throughout Strathmore, in the growing city of Dundee and all over Fife.

"They were awful thirsty folk, the Fife folk then. They would take as much drink as they could run across," an old smuggler said in the 1880s. His name was Sandy Knapp and he was well-known for his tales about the smuggling of bygone days - tales in which he himself played a substantial part.

It was a regular occurence for visitors to call on Auld Sandy in his isolated cottage in the glen to listen to the stories of olden times.

Always he would start his stories by bemoaning the changing face of the glen.

" Glenisla is no what it was at all," he would say, shaking his head as he told of the families who had gone, families who could count twenty and more generations in the area. " There's an awful change come over the glen since first I knew it," he would sigh but with the help of a sip or two of amber fluid it wasn't long before Sandy would regale his guests with tales of the wild days of his youth when jousting with the gaugers was a way of life

Tales of Whisky and Smuggling

for the entire population of the glen. Sitting there in traditional clothes of Scottish grey home-spun, a bright red cravat round his sturdy neck, Sandy would throw himself into his narrative with all the verve and enthusiasm of a man heir to a tradition of hundreds of years of storytelling.

And as he told his story by the peat fire in his humble cottage the visitors often felt that they too had been there when the glen was alive with people and the smell of peatreek filled the air.

" They were the cleverest and cunningest creatures I ever knew," he would say," and some of the very best were regulars at the Kirk. The minister himself knew fine what was going on, indeed he often helped those who had been fined for smuggling, the Reverend Burns - he was a fine man."

Like many a minister before him, Andrew Burns knew and appreciated the way his parishioners felt about making whisky. If they could make porridge from their own oats, why not whisky from their barley. They had always done so and could see no God-given reason to stop. These people were honest, hardworking and God-fearing and the minister agreed that there was little reason why they should change their ancient ways because of some government decision made hundreds of miles away - even if he couldn't say it openly. Luckily he was able to help those poor creatures unfortunate enough to be caught and fined for smuggling - none of the glen people had much in the way of possessions and finding the money for fines could land them in dire straits indeed.

Sitting one August day in the manse struggling with his sermon for the next Sunday service, the minister looked out of his window down the glen to the hotel. It was early afternoon and he could see a couple of familiar figures arrivng on horseback at the hotel. It was a couple of gaugers, Mackay and Whyte, on one of their visits. As they entered the hotel, the Reverend Burns put down his pen, rose and put on his coat.

"I'm just going up the glen for a wee wander" he called through to his wife who was busy in the kitchen, " I'll be back in a couple of hours."

Quickly he saddled his sturdy Highland garron (pony), mounted and rode slowly up the glen. As soon as he was out of sight of the hotel he urged the pony to a steady canter. There was work to be done. His job was to look after his flock and he did not wish to see any more of his parishoners brought into destitution by being forced to pay a fine for following their own traditions. An intelligent man, Burns was aware his own taste for peatreek would be seen by many as making him a hypocrite, and a criminal for helping the smugglers. However he knew his own mind and had made his peace with God on this issue. There was no doubt in his mind that his responsibility was to the people of the parish and not the distant government all those miles away in the south of England.

Up Glenisla

At every cottage that he passed the minister would take off his hat, wave it over his head and shout at the top of his voice," The Philistines be upon thee, Samson."

The effect was instantaneous. Either someone would dash from the cottage into the hills beyond, or a flurry of activity would take place to disguise the various processes going on in the preparation of barley.

" God, bless you minister," or, " Right you are Mr. Burns, " the replies would come as the minister rode on up the glen. The further up the glen he rode the wilder it became, with the neat gardens and fields of the valley floor giving way to the heather and tree-clad slopes of the mountains - the ravines and hollows providing perfect cover for the craftily constructed bothies containing the sma' stills. Going straight up the glen through Brewlands and Forter and on past Crandart and Dalnamer till he came to Auchavon, the minister managed to shout his warning at more than a dozen bothies all busy with the only industry capable of making them cash - smuggling. Known and trusted throughout the area the Reverend Burns knew most of the bothies in his parish and by the time the gaugers had left the hotel and headed north, the whole glen knew of the approach of the government men and appropriate action had been taken.

At Dalvanie Mary Cameron heard the Minister's call and right away sent her youngest, Archie up the slopes of Carn an Fhidleir to where his father was busy making peatreek. On hearing the news Geordie Cameron put out the fire and sent Archie and James, his eldest son who worked the bothy with him, back down with clear instructions. As the gaugers came into Dalvanie they saw a figure spring up from the heather on their left and run up Glen Beanie clutching a flagon. They took off after the man. Now James Cameron was a small lad, but he was known as a grand runner and as he was chased through the heather he kept a fair distance between himself and the mounted gaugers who had to be careful on the rough ground. However after ten minutes or so they were almost upon him. Suddenly the young man stopped and turned round, forcing the gaugers to pull up short and almost unseating Mackay.

" Right you," cried Whyte ," hand over that flagon in the King's name."

James did so and as he took it Whyte realised by its weight that it was empty.

"You damned smuggler brat," he roared," you are under arrest."

" Is that right? "replied James quietly," and what exactly will the charge be? Running through the heather?"

"You insolent young swine," Mackay said through gritted teeth,' we know what you are up to."

" But will you be arresting me then?" called James as the gaugers turned to ride back to Dalvanie, knowing they had been lured away by the oldest

45

trick in the book. As they furiously headed back towards the clachan (hamlet) they could hear the young man's laughter behind them. By the time they reached the cottages, Geordie Cameron himself was there, smiling and polite.

" Good-day officers, is there anything I can be doing for you.'

Without a word the gaugers left and headed up the glen.

A little further up the glen, the gaugers saw the slight figure of the Reverend Burns coming down the glen leading his garron by the bridle. As they passed he wished them a good day but all he got in reply was a grunt. The gaugers had already formed a suspicion that their day was going to be unsuccessful - like so many other occasions in Glenisla before.

By the time they got to Crandart they were in a temper and proceeded to search the small group of cottages roughly. They stuck their swords and long searching sticks into bedding, thatch and even into manure piles while the inhabitants of the wee clachan quietly watched.

Whyte in particular was in a foul mood. Standing in the kitchen of Willie Robertson's cottar-house he roared, " In the King's name, where have you hidden your contraband. I know you have illicit spirits in this house."

Willie looked straight at the officer, " I have no idea what you are talking about, sir," he said. Although he appeared calm, he was getting worried. This great oaf of a gauger was standing just inches from a wooden trapdoor under the straw that covered the whole floor - an earthen floor like all highland cottages. He was so angry he might even stamp his feet - and if he stamped on wood, the game would be up. In a carefully constructed cellar Willie had several dozen gallons of his own and his neighbours' manufacture.

"You know fine well what I am talking about Robertson, and I tell you this," the gauger's voice had gone quiet," we'll clean out this whole damn glen of you damned smugglers, your time is coming. Come on Mackay." The gauger abruptly turned and walked out of the kitchen followed by his partner. As they heard the revenue men mount and ride away there was a combined sigh of relief from the Robertson family.

" That was a close one, father I thought he was going to stamp on the trapdoor," said Niall, the elder son, a solidly-built lad in his late teens. "Aye you're right son. I'm thinking we'll maybe need to make ourselves a new hidey-hole, they'll be back soon, but not soon enough," he laughed. "We'll bring the run forward to tonight and our peatreek will be well away before we see those devils again."

All up the glen, fires were being doused in bothies, barley and malt were being carefully hidden and all signs of the main industry of Glenisla were out of sight before the unlucky gaugers arrived.

At Dalnamer Iain MacMillan had been spreading malt on his barn floor when word came that the gaugers were in the glen. Calling in his neighbours from the other three cottages in the clachan they began at once to spread straw all over the newly-turned malt. By the time the increasingly frustrated gaugers arrived there was no sign of the malt. Close by the small hamlet was a building known as a sheep-cot where orphan lambs and other sickly creatures were sheltered and looked after. The gaugers made for the sheep-cot, hoping that there would be evidence of illicit distilling to be found - they had in fact found some peatreek and a worm, the spiral pipe of the still in which the spirit condensed, from a still the previous year in that same sheep-cot. The low building was in fact clean - too clean, thought Mackay, an idea beginning to form in his mind.

"Right," he said to Whyte as they came out of the sheep-cot, ' We'll find nothing here. Let's go."

"What?" demanded his companion," there's plenty more places to look, man, what are you thinking of?"

" Never mind that,' snapped Mackay," I've seen enough, let's go." Saying this he mounted his horse and rode off, leaving Whyte little option but to follow him.

Soon the raging Whyte caught up with his fellow gauger and, grabbing Mackay's mount's bridle, forced him to pull up. Before he could speak however Mackay whispered, "Don't get too angry. I have a plan. The Supervisor will be delighted with it I'm certain. Just trust me Whyte, I know what I am doing."

Reluctantly Whyte calmed down and the two gaugers at once broke into a canter and headed back down the glen leaving the bemused inhabitants puzzling over their actions.

As he watched them go MacMillan looked thoughtful." There's something up," he said to his neighbours, " I think we'd better be a bit careful for a while."

A few hours later Mackay and Whyte were in the office of Supervisor McLeod in Coupar Angus.

" Well you have returned empty-handed again have you?" demanded the hot-tempered, burly revenue man.

" Eh, yes we have but we have a plan,' replied Mackay.

" A plan? A plan is it? Do let me in on your secret," the Officer said sarcastically.

" Well sir, we think that the sheep-cot at Dalnamer is being used for storing illicit spirits sir." said Mackay.

Tales of Whisky and Smuggling

" That's brilliant, man, just brilliant. My God we know every single one of that Dalnamer crew are making whisky and you tell me they store it there - that's just brilliant," he went on.

" Yes sir, but please listen," asked Mackay.

" All right, get on with it," snapped McLeod.

" Well the cot was far too clean to have been in use for animals sir, so we think it's been got ready for gathering the spirits for another run. Whyte and I thought," at this point he gave a sidelong glance at his companion,"we thought that we could come upon them by night when they would have no chance of seeing us coming."

" That's right sir," Whyte burst in, anxious to share in some of the credit for the plan," we could go up Glen Prosen and come down upon them from the hills."

" Hm, maybe it could work," mused McLeod. " Yes it's worth a try. Right we'll organise it for tomorrow night. We'll smash the ring at Dalnamer and with a bit of luck one of them might talk and let us get some more of these damned criminals. Even without that it'll put the rest of that horde of devils off their evil business for a while."

The following night the people of Dalnamer were rudely wakened at midnight by a terrible noise. A dozen gaugers and a small detachment of dragoons, led by McLeod, had ridden quietly down from the hills and as they approached the small group of simple Highland cottages had broken into a gallop and started yelling and firing their pistols. MacMillan flew from his bed and grabbing a stout oak cudgel threw open his door. In the area between the cottages he saw more than a dozen mounted men milling about, some carrying lighted brands. And there directly before him, looking down from his horse was Supervisor McLeod.

"Right then you damned smuggler, drop that stick in the King's name or I'll arrest you for assault."

Realising the seriousness of the situation, MacMillan dropped his cudgel, noticing as he did so that his neighbours were all at their own doors.

" Don't worry lads, it's only the King's Revenue Officers come to drag innocent crofters from their beds," he shouted,

" Innocent is it, you damned blackguard? I'll have you in jail by morning you smuggling swine," roared McLeod. " Right men," he went on, "you know what to do. Get on with it."

Watched by the dragoons, the gaugers dismounted and split into two groups some going to the corn-stacks and some to the sheep-cot. Kicking in the door, the first two went in carrying torches. Within seconds they were out again.

"There's nothing there, sir," they called.

" What?" McLeod shouted and, dismounting, ran into the cot. It was bare.

By now another gauger returned from the corn-stacks to report the same.

" Search the houses," trumpeted McLeod. " There's illicit whisky here someplace."

By now all of the inhabitants of Dalnamer were out of their beds and standing before their humble dwellings. Roughly shoving women and children aside, the gaugers proceeded to search every inch of the clachan, breaking furniture and utensils as they went. Nothing was found. McLeod was almost speechless with anger and frustration. His men and the dragoons were the same. They had made a long, arduous, roundabout journey to come upon these smugglers in total surprise, yet not one piece of incriminating evidence had been found.

"Right, right, you... you Highland devils," spluttered McLeod," you'll not store any more of your foul brew in that damned sheep cot. Fire it men."

At once a group of the gaugers began gathering peats and heather and piling it round the cot. Then they set fire to the material.

The turf and wood building burst into flame. Sparks began to fly towards the cottages. This was going too far. MacMillan and his neighbours headed to the sheep-cot to try and dowse the fire. Suddenly before them rode a Sergeant of Dragoons pointing his drawn sword directly at MacMillan.

" Leave it alone, smuggler ," he growled.

As soon as he was sure the cot could not be saved, McLeod gathered his men and they rode off, trampling what was left of the hay ricks as they went. The people of Dalnamer were busy emptying their houses of all their belongings as the sparks from the fire threatened to set their thatched homes ablaze. Luckily the wind shifted and their houses were saved.

Iain MacMillan's canny awareness that something was up when the gaugers had left the previous time had paid off. All of the Dalnamer peatreek was safely stored in a bothy in the hills. But this treatment at the hands of the Excisemen was too much. The Dalnamer people had almost lost everything. They had their whisky, but what right had McLeod to behave in that way, they asked themselves. No right - he had acted as if he was above the law. Something should be done about it.

" Enough, enough," MacMillan said to the furious gathering, swollen by neighbours who had heard the noise, seen the flames and come from nearby clachans. "Tomorrow we can talk about it. Let's all to bed."

The following day, though MacMillan himself had calmed down and was happy to have saved the peatreek, his neighbours were still incensed at the high-handed treament meted out by Supervisor McLeod. They had long memories and would not forget the gaugers' excesses but they did not want to let this insult pass unnoticed. Accordingly a letter was drafted to the local

Tales of Whisky and Smuggling

Justice of the Peace, a copy of which has survived.

Dalnamer.

To his Majesty's Justice of the piece, Collector of Excise and gentlemen of the County -

We, the poor pendiculars in Dalnamer, in Glenisla, doth find ourselves under the Disagreeable deedsesity of giving you our complaint on the misconduct of a party of Exise and Dragouns that came to our Countray on the neight of August 30th under the command of McLoud, Supervisor in Couparangus, who came not as Exise, But as plunderers and thieves of the neight. they went to our stack yeards and pulled down our corn stacks, fastened there horses to the number of Eleven, they thrang more of our Corn before them than was sufficient for six times the number.

They then went to a sheep cote, where they had some time before found some smuggled stuff, and when not finding anything belonging smuggling, they went to the said sheep cote carrying peats and hether to it, and then set it aburning, which, had it not been the goodness of providence in turning the wind from the north to the north-east our whole houses, ourselves, Wives, and Children, along with our corn and cattle, being in the Dead of neight, had all been burned to ashes.

What the monsters' desire was we know not, only they could have no grounds for so base an action, nor doth the Laws of our Countray alow such practises, and if the county gentlemen dos not pay, or cause to be pay'd, the Loss of our corn, of course we must aplay to the fiscal of thee county to look after such thifts and volinces.

True, there were smugglars in our countray, yet such as was cannot be robed by the Exise - nor do we deserve such usag from them, for had they call'd on us, and asked it of us, we would have given them as at other times, meat for themselves and corn or hay for there horses. But in place of that the Serjeant of Dragouns threatened us with a drawn sword in his hand, that if we said aney more about our corn he would setesfy himself with our blood.

So if the fiscal of the county doth not put a stope to such Barbarus practices, Blood for Blood must be allowed.

Despite the call at the end of the letter for a return to the ancient Highland practice of feuding the Glenisla folk soon calmed down and the letter seems not to have been sent. However the bad feeling towards the gaugers did not decrease and there were many instances of the Glenisla men taking delight in making the gaugers look like fools in the ensuing years. And if occasionally a blow went in a little harder in the scuffles that arose between the combatants in the perpetual war against peatreek, well the Glenisla men felt they had just cause.

As Auld Sandy finished his tale about the Glenisla smugglers he stopped and looked into the fire glowing in the grate.

" For all that there was sometimes bad blood between us and the gaugers," he mused, " there were many of them who liked a drop too. I mind what my father use to say of his brother Charlie, a man that liked the peatreek well. He used to say when he had had one dram he was fine, when he had two he was tremendous, but when he had three he hadn't had half enough." Laughing quietly, the old man finished, " Aye it was grand stuff we made in the old times, and you don't see its like these days." Then looking up with a merry twinkle in his clear grey eyes he added, " well, not that often."

Glendaruel

Nestling in the hills of Cowal and running parallel to Loch Fyne is the bonny, curved glen where the river Ruel runs - Glendaruel. Here as in all the Highlands the local people round the turn of the nineteenth century were actively involved in the distillation of the peatreek. Times were generally hard and the subsistence farming of most of the people left them little possibility of raising any cash crops other than whisky. A combination of tradition, necessity and a liking for the *cratur* made making whisky an amost universal occupation. In addition the leftovers or draff made a nutritious cattle food, a bonus much appreciated by the crofters. The local Justices of the Peace throughout Scotland appreciated the contribution the industry made to the cash economy as well as the quality of the home-grown produce, and were rarely as severe in their judgements and fines as the Supervisors of Excise would wish. Many a blind eye was turned in mansion and manse to the peatreek industry. Glendaruel was no different.

Although the possibility of having "a gauger in every glen" had been discussed by the powers that be at the excise in London they had wisely decided against such a policy. A lone gauger would be open to all sorts of bribery and corruption and there would be no way of guaranteeing the safety of such men. They tended to be gathered into local county towns under the control of a Supervisor and often had extensive areas to look after. The nearest Supervisor to Glendaruel was at Lochgilphead on the other side of Loch Fyne. To visit the glen they had to cross Loch Fyne to Otter on the ferry (or come secretly in a navy boat) then come over the 1,000 foot pass on Cruach nan Tarbh (The Bull's Peatstack) and down into Glendaruel itself. As the busiest time for making whisky was always the winter the gaugers could have a tough time just getting to places like Glendaruel to try and do their job.

Glendaruel

In the early years of the 19th century there was a "clachan school" at Ballochandroin where the road from Otter came down into Glendaruel. This type of school was common throughout Scotland, the long tradition of respect for learning ensured that wherever there were enough children a teacher would be hired and a school would be founded. Often enough the teachers were paid in kind and lived much as the glenfolk themselves did. They were always treated with great respect and had a position of some status in the community. This particular school however had a function other than education. The *dominie* , or teacher, Mr. Lamont had been brought up in Cowal and was well aware that the majority of the parents of his class were involved in the peatreek industry. The busy seaports of the Clyde provided them with a market and the industry was often their only means of raising cash. By this period many rents had to be paid in cash and selling whisky was a good a means as any other of raising it. So Mr. Lamont, who enjoyed an occasional drop of the *cratur* himself took advantage of the school's position. After a few years in the job he knew the general whereabouts of most stills and who ran them. More than once he had helped out in the bothies. He therefore set up the Glendaruel early warning system - a system of great simplicity and effectiveness.

If any group of gaugers came to Glendaruel from the Otter ferry they had to come through the pass over Cruach nan Tarbh and into the glen by the clachan school. If the schoolteacher didn't notice them, one of the pupils certainly would. Certainly they wouldn't go unnoticed. As soon as they were seen Lamont would spring into action.

" Right, Willie, Seumas, Mairi, Geordie, Shona, Catriona off you go. Tell your parents the Government men are in the glen again," he would order. Immediately the gaugers were past the school, out would pour the excited children heading with all the speed of youth through shortcuts and byways to the nearest steadings and cottages. Here the second part of the strategy came into play. The Highlands had a long tradition of sending a messenger with the fiery cross, a simple cross of two sticks with one side of the crosspiece burnt and the other dipped in blood to summon the clan or to warn of danger. At each clachan a new runner would take over. However this was of limited value against mounted men who were intent on raiding not cattle, as in the olden days, but the lovingly tended sma' stills where the amber nectar of peatreek was made.

The method used was simple indeed. It was effective on any day but a Monday. As soon as they got the word that the gaugers were in the glen the women of the clachans and cottages near the school would hang up sheets and blankets as if they were drying them. The signs would be noticed in the next cottage or group of houses and the people there would immediately follow suit. In an ever widening circle up and down the glen the message was spread. Pausing only to hang out the signal, the womenfolk would head off to wherever the bothies were to inform the men what was happening. It was a peatreek semaphore of stunning simplicity and was used in glens and straths throughout Scotland.

However the gaugers were no fools and once in the glen would ride furiously for the location they had chosen before even leaving Lochgilphead. Long experience had taught them that if they delayed at all once they had arrived in the glen the locals would dowse the bothy fires and spirit away all the stills and peatreek. Speed was of the essence. With their need of fresh running water the bothies were built alongside the fast-running streams that ran down from the hills to feed the river in the plain of the glen. There are literally dozens of such streams in Glendaruel and in the early years of the nineteenth century most of them had at least one bothy alongside.

So despite the early warning system there were occasions when the Lochgilphead gaugers would come on a still where the fire still smoked, giving away its location. When this happened, the local people would gather at the still and attempt to defend it.

Wee Seumas MacLachlan was heading for his home at Lower Camchuart when he heard the horses thundering up behind him. Desperately he threw himself into the heather by the side of the path as the galloping gaugers passed. He hadn't made it in time. The gaugers would smash his father's still and maybe even arrest his father. As soon as the horses were passed the wee laddie picked himself up and ran after them. Soon three of the gaugers turned off up a narrow ravine to the left. The other three carried on towards Camchuart. However Seumas needn't have worried. The peatreek semaphore had done its work. By the time the three mounted gaugers turned to ride up the stream above Lower Camchuart a crowd of glen folk were between them and the still, a hundred yards up the course of the burn.

"Stand aside in the name of the king,' the leading gauger called out.

The only response was a shower of stones from the people ahead. Beyond the crowd the gaugers could clearly see MacLachlan and three of his neighbours dismantling his sma' still.

"MacLachlan you are under arrest in the King's name," the gauger yelled at the top of his voice. Another shower of stones came, forcing the gaugers back down the narrow glen. Up ahead MacLachlan and his friends were clamly dismantling the still. Again the gaugers tried to force their way up the narrow glen. They knew had to actually seize a still before they could bring charges. Again they were forced back. The glen was too narrow to allow them to manouevre their horses to full advantage. Within minutes MacLachlan and his friends had the still in pieces and were hurrying up the side of the hill as their families and friends formed a human barrier between them and the gaugers. Soon they were heading out of sight, secure in the knowledge that they were safe from prosecution.

"Damn you MacLachlan," the gauger shouted, " Come on lads," he called to his companions," let's go and see how the others have done."

They wheeled their horse and, with the jeers of the locals ringing in their ears they headed back down the glen to join their comrades. They had fared better.

In another ravine the other gaugers had managed to sieze the still of John MacEwan before a crowd had gathered to delay them. Once he realised that the capture of his still was inevitable John had calmly allowed the Excisemen to take it. He hadn't managed to get help to defend his still - this time.

From personal experience he knew what would follow. He would be sent a summons to appear at Lochgilphead before a court of local Justices of the Peace and he would doubtless be fined. The only way he would be able to pay the fine would be to set up another sma' still and begin distilling peatreek again. Och well, he would just have to pull his belt in for a while. It was a damned inconvenience but not a disaster.

A month or so later, John was standing before the court in the Supervisor of Excise's office in Lochgilphead. Before him were ranged five Justices of the Peace, landowners in the area. The chief magistrate was Alexander Lamont, whose lands encompassed the southern end of Glendaruel. The evidence had been heard. Three different gaugers had testified that they had siezed the still from the accused, who was trying to dismantle it as they came upon him. There was no doubt as to John's guilt. There remained however the matter of the fine. Lamont and his co-magistrates were all too aware of the contribution that peatreek made to the cash economy of the district. In fact they knew well that the majority of the money they received in rents from their tenants was raised by the sale of home-made peatreek to willing, thirsty customers in the towns and villages that bordered the Clyde. Much of the whisky went as far as Glasgow where the growing population of displaced Highland families provided a ready market.

Still, as Justices of the Peace they were charged with upholding the law. They could not turn a blind eye to smugglers when they appeared in court no matter what they did when on their own lands. John would have to be fined. The court was full with Glendaruel folk who had come over from Otter to see what would happen. Lamont held a whispered consultation with the other J.P.s. Geddes, the Supervisor of Excise watched fatalistically. As always, he had pressed for a severe fine, but he too knew the realities of the situation. MacEwan would get a small fine, and if he didn't have the cash his neighbours would pay it for him and he would have another still

Tales of Whisky and Smuggling

working within a week. The only consolation Geddes had was that he had also seized six gallons of freshly-distilled peatreek at MacEwan's still. The sale of that would more than cover the day's expenses, so he had had some wages from the escapade.

"Right MacEwan," Lamont sternly said, " you have been found guilty of breaking the Excise laws. We must have obedience to the law or we will slide into chaos. His Majesty's Government exists to benefit everyone in society and the laws it passes must be obeyed. You, sir, are a persistent offender. This is the third time that you have appeared before this court on a charge of smuggling. This illegal manufacture does great harm to the revenues of our civil government as well as threatening the moral fibre of our nation. You are therefore ordered to pay a fine of ten shillings."

A murmur went round the court. That wasn't too bad at all. Within minutes the fine was paid and the Glendaruel folk were heading for the ferry back to Otter. Once back they would have a collection to allow John MacEwan to invest in new equipment and within a few weeks he would repay his friends and neighbours. After a month or so it would be back to business as usual. The confiscated whisky would be sold by auction and the gauger would receive his cut. If there was no violence involved it was only when fines were unpaid that imprisonment was imposed as a sentence. The smugglers would band together to help any of their number who was fined particularly harshly.

At the same court another Glendaruel man William MacLachlan was charged with having more than the accepted amount of malt in his possession. The malt, sprouted and dried barley, was the basic material for the manufacture of the peatreek. Geddes had received information from an itinerant Irish packman that MacLachlan would be having his malt ground at the mill at Escaclachan on a certain day. So the gaugers had arrived and found the miller Mr. Moodie grinding malt for MacLachlan. The malt was siezed and taken to Lochgilphead where MacLachlan appeared and was also fined, in this case five shillings. However, though there was a ready market among publicans for confiscated peatreek - the quality being so much better than officially allowed spirits - the sale of malt was not quite so simple. The main market for it was for making peatreek!

A few days after the trial the confiscated malt was sold for a few shillings to Archibald MacAusland, farmer, of Maymore in Glendaruel. MacAusland loaded the malt onto his pony and took it to board the ferry at Ardrishaig to cross to Otter. There he saw a neighbour and friend of his who was waiting to board the ferry.

" Good day to you Willie. How are things with you today? " he said extending his hand.

" Hello yourself, Archie. I am well," his friend replied, shaking the offered hand vigourously. " Are you well yourself? "

" I am that," MacAusland went on. " I have just done something a bit daft though."

" And what would that be?" asked Willie.

" Well, I have just bought a couple of sacks of malt from the gaugers," Archie said, " and I have just realised that I have no real need of it at this time."

" Och, that's a great pity that," Willie said sympathetically, " but maybe I can help you Archie."

" And how is that Willie?" asked Macausland.

" Well it just so happens that I am in need of a couple of sacks of malt myself and if you would consider letting me buy it from you ... "

" Och Willie, you are a friend indeed. For helping me out I will let you have the malt for just what I paid the gaugers for it, if that is all right with you?" the farmer said quizzically.

" That would be just champion," replied Willie, " and it so happens I have young James waiting with the cart at Otter so I could take it right away."

" Right you are then, that's a bargain," MacAusland stated emphatically and the two men shook hands again.

So when the ferry docked at Otter William MacLachlan and his son James loaded the two bags of malt on his cart and drove off to put them to the good use they been had originally intended for. A few days later MacAusland found a fine big flagon outside his door, full to the brim with bright, clear Glendaruel peatreek.

Although there were logistical problems with the transporting of the peatreek, these were overcome by the combined efforts of the smugglers and their customers. Caught in the dark tenements of the towns and cities, living in cramped conditions with stale air and little light, the Highlanders could still take a dram of peatreek and dream of the bens and glens they had left behind them. And the Lowland people too knew the quality of peatreek far surpassed anything else available. There was a ready market for the produce of the smugglers and by a combination of application and ingenuity that market continued to be supplied. Try as they might, the gaugers were up against almost the entire population and could only hinder but never destroy the peatreek trade.

The situation changed when the government in London enacted a new law to help their allies the big distillers who found the competition from the peatreek too much. The act stated that any landowner or farmer would be

Tales of Whisky and Smuggling

heavily fined if any person at all was found distilling illicit spirits on land that they owned. The landowners' ignorance of any such activity was no defence. If smuggling took place on their lands, they were responsible. This change signalled the end of the peatreek as a major cottage industry throughout Scotland - a change that was accelerated by the ever-increasing clearances of Highland glens as these same landowners saw greater profit in sheep and deer than in people.

However there are stories that refer to as many as half-a-dozen stills producing high-quality peatreek in the early years of this century in remote bothies in Cowal. Today's available range of single malts and blended whiskies surely provides for all tastes, the quality far surpassing what used to be on sale. However the spirit of independence of the Celtic Scot has not entirely disappeared and that spirit may still made manifest from the juice of the barley in various locations. The quality of such spirit is said to be truly magnificent but sadly the author cannot pass comment, never having tasted it.

The Poor Minister

Inverness, the capital of the Highlands was a great centre of peatreek activity during our period. Although there had been clearances the glens and valleys of the surrounding areas were still well occupied and the natives were keen on their whisky. As has been noted, the people of Strathglass and the Aird were particularly active in peatreek manufacture. This activity was also widespread among their neighbours in the Black Isle the beautiful peninsula that lies between the Beauly and Cromarty Firths - an area of prime importance to the ancient Picts, which also overlooks Nigg Bay where there has been so much activity and development related to the discovery of North Sea oil. The people here are charming and hospitable, always polite and helpful - in fact they are the true heirs to the ancient Highland traditions of hospitality and honour.

However in the heyday of the peatreek there were other aspects of the Highland character which seem to have been much more to the fore - independence and the capacity for physical struggle.

It wasn't just the menfolk who were prepared to resist the gaugers. The women were as involved in the business as their men and as keen to protect their investment of time and effort.

One summer's day in 1816 gauger John Proudfoot was out on horseback looking around in the southern part of the Black Isle not far from Redcastle on the Beauly Firth. He was coming to the farm of Braes of Grogaston when he noticed a couple of sacks by a dyke in a field. There was no one to be seen. Immediately he dismounted and crossed the field to look at the sacks. Taking out his clasp-knife he cut the twine holding the top of the first sack together. As he had suspected it was malted barley, ready to be used to make peatreek. At first he thought of hiding nearby and following whoever came to pick up the malt but he couldn't be sure of making an arrest on his own. The local people were known to be quite prepared to defend themselves and their property against the revenue men. So, thinking a bird in the hand was better than two in the bush, he decided to go and borrow a cart to transport the malt back to the Supervisor's office in Inverness, a bit over a dozen miles away.

Riding into the nearby farm of Braes of Grogaston, Proudfoot dismounted and knocked at the farmhouse door. The door was opened by the tenant farmer, William Leitch, a tall, dark-haired man of about sixty.

" Good day to you sir," said Proudfoot. " I am John Proudfoot of his Majesty's Excise and I wish to have the use of a cart."

"Good day to you," replied Leitch. " It's a cart you're wanting is it? "

" You will be recompensed, if you write to the Supervisor's office in Inverness," Proudfoot went on." It will be returned to you within a day or two."

" That's as may be, but what is it you will be wanting the cart for?" asked Leitch.

"I have found two bags of malt which I believe are intended for the illicit distillation of spirits, so I am confiscating them," said Proudfoot stiffly. " They are in a field over there," he said, pointing. " Do you know anything of them?"

"What me? No, no, they are not mine," Leitch protested, " I wonder whose they are."

"Look man," said Proudfoot, " will you loan me a cart or not? I am on the King's business and I do not wish to tarry."

" All right Mr. Proudfoot, I will get you a cart. Will you be using your own horse to pull it?"

" Don't be stupid man, this isn't a cart-horse," spluttered Proudfoot.

"Just so, just so," said Leitch as he casually went to organise a horse and cart for the gauger. While he was talking to the gauger a small boy had come out of the farm-house's back door and was heading off to a nearby group of cottages. Leitch leisurely hitched up a horse and cart and after going over the precise address he should write to for recompense with the exciseman, eventually handed him the cart and horse and watched him drive out of the farmyard.

By the time the gauger had driven to where the sacks of malt were, a crowd of about a dozen women had arrived on the scene. The leader of these women appeared to be Margaret McLennan, a stout, red-haired woman, in her early thirties. As the gauger moved to get the first sack of malt, McLennan and Janet Young, a somewhat younger, fair-haired woman, grabbed the horse and began to unyoke it.

" Leave that horse alone," Proudfoot shouted.

" Is it your horse then?" replied Margaret.

" You know fine I am on the King's business woman. Now unhand that horse," barked Proudfoot.

" I know no such thing ," said Margaret coming to stand directly in front of the gauger, her hands on her hips and a hard gleam in her eye. " Maybe you're a thief stealing these sacks there."

" You insolent besom, stand aside," roared Proudfoot as a couple of the other women began to lead the uhitched horse away, " Come back with that horse you," he shouted after the other women. As they led the horse away the remaining women formed a barrier between it and Proudfoot. " You are a bunch of criminals. You are interfering with an officer of His Majesty's Excise . You know whose malt this is, don't you?, " he shouted. " That's why you are doing this. Whose malt is it?" he almost screamed, his face inches from that of Margaret MacLennan.

" I don't know whose malt this is," replied Maggie, standing her ground, "but I'll tell you what. We'll let you have the malt."

The gauger stood back, surprised at this sudden change.

" All we want is the sacks," said Maggie as her friends burst into loud laughter.

At this, Proudfoot whirled round, took out his clasp-knife and in one movement opened it up and ripped it through one of the bags of malt. Picking it up he began to scatter the contents over the field. For a moment the women stood still, then Maggie MacLennan bent down, picked up a smallish stone and hurled it at the gauger. She missed by a yard, but the missile was followed by others thrown by the rest of the women. Dropping the part-emptied sack Proudfoot took to his heels, doubling back once he was out of the women's throwing range to head after his horse.

Running after his horse back towards Grogaston, with Maggie MacLennan, Janet Young and the others coming after him Proudfoot was beginning to get worried. At that point he saw Donald Noble, a fellow gauger, riding towards him.

" Quick Donald," he shouted, " give me a hand up."

Soon the two gaugers were on the horse and heading back towards William Leitch's farm. Arriving there, both dismounted and Proudfoot burst into the farmhouse. Addressing Leitch, he barked, " Right man, have you any firearms? We are being attacked by a mob and we are about the King's business. Quickly man, do you have any firearms?" By now they could hear the yelling women approaching the farmhouse.

" Och I am sorry, sir, but we have no firearms here at all," said Leitch, clearly unworried by the way things were developing.

" Damn it," spat Proudfoot, then, noticing a pair of thick wooden staves behind the farmhouse door, he grabbed them, handed one to Noble and ran

Tales of Whisky and Smuggling

back outside, just as the women enetered the farmyard. In the lead was
Maggie MacLennan. Running straight at her he whacked her across the
head. With a scream of " Murder!" Maggie collapsed in a heap. For a
moment the others stood still. Then they came at the gauger. As they closed
on him, Proudfoot ran into a barn and bolted the door. Noble had wisely
stayed inside the farmhouse. The women began to hammer on the barn door,
shouting curses at the imprisoned gauger. By now word of the gaugers'
presence had spread and Maggie's husband John and his friend Calum
Campbell soon arrived on the scene.

It did not take the men long to find their way into the barn . After a short
struggle they had Proudfoot tightly bound. Noble decided to keep out of the
way and stayed in the farmhouse. Proudfoot had attacked the woman, not
him, and anyway discretion was the better part of valour, he told himself.
From his hiding place in a cupboard he heard some of the women bring the
bloodstained form of Maggie MacLennan into the farmhouse kitchen and lay
her on the table. She was still breathing but all agreed she looked terrible.
" Right," said Janet Young, raising her voice above the others, " let's take
this damned gauger swine into Inverness to the Sheriff and have him tried
for murder."
A chorus of assent was interrupted by John MacLennan who had come in
and was kneeling by his wife, saying, " She's still breathing, fetch the doctor."
Soon a further decision was made. They would take Proudfoot before the
sheriff the next day as it was now too late to get to Inverness before nightfall.
Again taking the lead, Janet Young said, " Let's put him in the pond down
by the dunghill till we are ready for him in the morning."
This suggestion was met with universal approval and while MacLennan
tended his wife the women dragged the unfortunate gauger down to the
pond and threw him in. The pond was only two or three feet deep so if he
kept on his knees, Proudfoot would be in no danger of drowning.
" He'll keep till morning," Janet said, " Let's all be going home till then.'
As the women dispersed William Leitch was watching from a little way
off with his neighbour James Stuart, another successful tenant farmer. They
were prepared to help dodge the gaugers but they realised assaulting one of
them was a different matter, and sure to be frowned on by the magistrates.
Once night had fallen, these two returned with Noble and freed the sorry
gauger from his plight. With Noble's help, Proudfoot managed to find his
horse, though without a saddle, and the pair of them rode off to Inverness.
In the morning the women found Proudfoot gone and realised they
would have problems in bringing charges against him now. Proudfoot,
however, had been busy. That same day he had warrants taken out against as
many of the women whose names he and Noble could recall.

The result of all this was that on September 27th Maggie Maclennan, recovered, but still showing bruises, Janet Young, Calum Campbell and half-a dozen of the other women appeared before Inverness District Sheriff Court. The charges included assault on a revenue officer, mobbing and rioting. John MacLennan and Anne Fraser hadn't turned up at court and were outlawed for not appearing.

Because of the seriousness of the charges it was a jury trial. There could be little doubt as to the outcome. The testimony of Leitch's wife Helen had some effect when she described Proudfoot's assault on Maggie MacLennan. The jury found them all guilty but asked for mercy for Maggie because of her injuries - she had spent two weeks in bed recovering. Accordingly she was only fined but Janet Young, Campbell and four other women were jailed for thirty days.

Not all of the clashes between gaugers and smugglers round about the Aird were as brutal as this. The Sheriff, charged with upholding the law had to be seen to give support to the gaugers but sometimes the gaugers themselves were capable of exercising discretion.

Now, the minister at Kiltarity in The Aird about this time was Alisdair Hutcheson, a kind and understanding man, much respected by his parishioners. However to the Laird, the minister was much as other men and had to pay his rent. His stipend was small and from the day he had taken over his position the minister had been hard-pressed to find the necessary cash to pay the rent for his manse and the glebelands, as the land allotted to ministers was known. It was normal practice for ministers to grow as much food as possible on the glebelands to feed themselves and their families. There were always occasional gifts from parishioners to help out but these were invariably in the form of food or clothing and did nothing to increase any minister's cash income.

With a growing family to feed, Alisdair's plight did not improve as the years passed.

He gave the matter great thought. How did his parishioners manage? Few of them had acess to cash - except by making peatreek. He needed cash and he was lucky enough to have quite extensive glebelands. That land could grow barley and from barley he too could manufacture whisky! After all hadn't his father and his father's father before him made their own *uisge beatha*? Poor Alisdair had a long, hard struggle with his conscience over this matter. In the end, considering that his duty was to serve God rather than government and because cash was in such terrible short supply, he decided he had little option. So the minister entered the peatreek trade. He had quietened his conscience but being a canny individual he would pray to God

Tales of Whisky and Smuggling

every night before going to bed that he would not be discovered by the temporal authorities. He was a dedicated minister, and well respected by his flock, but he knew fine well that if discovered he would probably be prosecuted and this would mean being dismissed from his position. Serving the needs of his flock was one thing but the respectability of the Kirk was another. Ministers were expected to uphold the law and support the power of government but Alisdair was sure that no one in his congregation would draw attention to the fact that their minister never railed against the smuggling trade. Most of them were either involved themselves or had someone in their family who was active in the business.

So the minister began to manufacture peatreek, setting up a still not far from the manse on the edge of Boblainy Forest. Discreetly asking around he soon had several outlets for his produce, which was of excellent quality. A careful and fastidious man in all things, Alisdair studied his craft and his endeavours bore fruit in the quality of the whisky he made. One of his regular customers was the publican of the Star Inn in Invernesss, a somewhat boorish individual by the name of James Shanks, who never had a good word to say for anyone. He was also extremely mean and though he knew that Alisdair's peatreek was of superb quality he was always trying to beat his price down. He had tried to hint to the minister that he was in a particularly dangerous situation because of his calling - in fact he was trying to blackmail the minister. However Alisdair saw good in all men and was unaware of the meaning of Shanks' hints. A more worldly man would have realised his danger but Alisdair was blissfully unaware of the danger he was in from Shanks.

After several attempts at getting the minister to accept less Shanks met the same reply each time . " A fair day's wage for a fair day's labour, James. You know how hard I work and I certainly have no intention, or chance, of becoming a rich man. We'll just stick to the agreed price. Thank you and may God bless you." The mean-spirited Shanks grew more and more frustrated with this criminal minister who pretended such an air of innocence. He couldn't really conceive of Alisdair being sincere for he saw everything in life in terms of profit and loss - money was his god.

At last, he had had enough and decided to inform the gaugers that a smuggler would be approaching the Clachnaharry Inn at a certain time one Monday night after dark. For some strange reason he couldn't quite bring himself to say that the smuggler was a man of the cloth.

Unaware of the hovering cloud of danger Alisdair had as usual taken his cart to the still, loaded it with several flagons of his best, covered them up with peats and headed for his regular meeting with Shanks. It was a mild night and he was thinking over the previous Sunday's sermon as he passed

Clachnaharry. When he was a few hundred yards past the village a figure stepped out of the darkness and ordered him to stop in the King's name. It was gauger Hossack, a man relatively new to Inverness and he didn't recognise the minister.

" Where are you going at this time of the night?" demanded the gauger.

" Eh, I am going into town with my peats," stammered Alisdair, saying to himself he wasn't telling a lie - the cart did have peats in it and maybe the man would let him pass. Suddenly, however, all he could think of was the quotation, " Render unto God that which is God's, and render unto Caesar that which is Caesar's".

"To town with your peats eh?," the gauger went on, " well I'll just have a look."

So saying, he stepped forward, and unshading the lantern in his hand, proceeded to rummage among the peats. In seconds he had uncovered one, two, three, four and at last five flagons of the finest peatreek.

" What's this then?" he demanded of the by now shaking Alisdair.

" O Lord, Thou has betrayed Thy servant at last," Alisdair burst out.

The gauger stepped forward to have a closer look at this apparently devout smuggler who was now holding his head in his hands. He had heard many responses from smugglers on being stopped but never any like this. In the light he saw the dark clothes of the driver, of a different cut and material from normal homespun. A thought began to form in the gauger's mind. No it couldn't be. Impossible.

He was still standing with his lantern held high when Alisdair, taking a deep breath, blurted out, " Yes, you are right, it is whisky. I am guilty of smuggling. O Lord, I am a sinner and deserve judgement. I am the Reverend Alisdair Hutcheson of Kiltarlity and I distilled these spirits illicitly, God have mercy upon me."

Hossack's jaw dropped. A minister! No it couldn't be, it must be a trick, it had to be.

" Um well, tell me then why would a minister be involved in making and selling whisky against the law then?" he asked.

In a state of shock at having his worst fears realised, Alisdair proceeded to unburden himself to the revenue officer. How he needed the money to pay his rent, his stipend being totally used to feed his family, how he had set up his still using knowledge gathered as a youth, where the still was - on and on the minister went, pouring out his guilt.

" Enough Sir, enough," Hossack said at last. " Will you tell me where you were taking this stuff please?"

Having said so much Alisdair told him this as well, sure that Shanks couldn't be arrested for intending to have peatreek delivered.

Tales of Whisky and Smuggling

" I see," Hossack mused. He knew Shanks and did not like the man. " Tell me have you ever had any bother with this Shanks? He strikes me as an unpleasant character."

" Och, no, no," replied Alisadair," apart from his always trying to make me charge less - which in conscience I could hardly do - I make only enough for the rent from this you know. I knew it was wrong. Whatever will become of my family now?"

Hossack was standing there looking thoughtful as the minister spoke, clearly trying to make up his mind about something.

" Look sir," he eventually spoke. " Will you give me your word as a minister of religion that you will destroy your still and stop making whisky forever if I let you go on your way?"

"What?" asked the astonished Alisdair.

" If I let you pass with your whisky, and you go sell it to Shanks, I want your word that this will be the last time and that you will detroy your still tonight when you go home and never make whisky again," the gauger told him.

" Certainly, if that is what you wish me to do," replied a thoroughly bemused Alisdair."

"Right then on you go, and make sure you keep your word sir," finished Hossack, drawing the shade over his lantern and stepping off the road into the darkness before Alisdair could even say, 'thank you'.

Doing as he had been told, Alisdair went to the Inn and completed his transaction with Shanks as quickly as possible. He was in such a hurry to be off he did not notice the look of confusion on Shanks' face. The minister had never seemed so businesslike before. Taking the agreed amount as before, Alisdair headed back to destroy his still, never once looking behind him. He could not work out why the gauger had acted as he had but he was sensible enough to count his blessings and do as he had promised. Never again would the Kiltarlity Minister tend his mash or watch his spirits run clear. He was finished with the peatreek forever. As he headed home, he gave a prayer of thanks for his deliverance.

Back at the Clachnaharry Inn, Shanks was just about to fill some bottles from the first flagon when a knock came at the Inn door.

Opening it he saw gauger Hossack, lantern held high in one hand. Hossack spoke: "I am here in the King's name. I have reason to believe you have illicit spirits in this place. Ah, there, behind you: flagons of fresh peatreek I think. I am confiscating these on behalf of His Majesty's Excise and you, James Shanks, will be summonsed for being in possession of these spirits contrary to law."

After that night Alisdair Hutcheson never again made peatreek. He managed to get by, and his popularity amongst his flock increased as the time he had been giving to making peatreek he now devoted to his parishioners. As word had got around of the dirty trick Shanks had tried to play on the unworldly minister, custom at the Star Inn dropped off. And with gauger Hossack keeping such a close eye on him after this, it was only a matter of months before he sold up and moved back south.

A Tragic Feud

In the early nineteenth century, the industry was so widespread and accepted among rural communities that many gaugers and even Supervisors of Excise were sympathetic to the smugglers. Many a time such men would find a fine salmon or basket of trout on their doorstep, tokens of appreciation from smugglers. Turning a blind eye was the norm among the landowning classes and many of the magistrates. It could even be argued that the smuggling industry delayed that greatest of curses - the clearances. By providing a ready source of cash, the smuggling trade undoubtedly kept many people on the land who otherwise would have been driven away by poverty, as the Lairds turned to raising money from sheep.

In many areas, smugglers and gaugers helped each other. If the gaugers let the smugglers operate then there would be occasional finds of whisky and stills - though often these stills would be worn out or of low quality. The cheapest stills were made of tin and when the gaugers discovered them they would simply pierce them through with a sword or a 'finder' - a long pole with a pointed metal tip for pushing into hay stacks, peat stacks and for testing for hidden chambers under floors or among the heather. The piercing of such tin mash tubs etc. had a handy spin off for another rural industry. Because such stills were of low quality, once pierced they weren't worth being carted off, so they were usually left where they were found. The smuggler would then simply hire a tinker to come and repair the still, giving work to the tinker and getting the still back in production.

The industry was so developed that the sight of whole convoys of smugglers or "flaskers" was a common sight. The term flaskers came form the large tin flasks of whisky that were used by many Highland smugglers to transport their wares in the West. These flasks were cheaper and easier to replace than wooden "ankers" or small barrels and making them kept many a tinker busy. Such convoys were a common sight round Aberfoyle and the Trossachs as smugglers from all over the Highlands made their way towards

Glasgow, where displaced Gaels provided a regular and thirsty market. Some of these convoys had as many as sixty whisky-laden ponies and there are reports of them being preceded by pipers, even into the city itself.

The organisers of such convoys obviously had good intelligence about the gaugers' whereabouts or were in collusion with them. However, not all the Excisemen were "in cahoots" with smugglers and in order to try and combat the large-scale transportation the Excise had appointed Rangers - gaugers who could roam as far and wide as they found necessary, and who could call for assistance on any local Supervisor.

Smugglers were active in most parts of Scotland, and the area round Aberfoyle was no exception. Not all of the smugglers were poor crofters or tenant farmers either. Some of them were relatively wealthy people. One such was James MacFarlane, a cattle dealer from Aberfoyle. He was successful at his trade and had several employees. MacFarlane himself had a taste for peatreek, which he had developed early. In fact his father and grandfather had been active in making *poit dubh*. Having known the best from his youth, it was little suprise that MacFarlane preferred the real stuff in his more mature years.

James MacFarlane was a proud man, proud of his Highland heritage and of the success he had had in his chosen business. He was aware of his position in the community and had no wish to be considered anything other than a respectable businessman. He therefore was extremely careful about his smuggling activities. He rented lands in various areas around Aberfoyle, where he kept cattle, and one of these areas was at the foot of Craigmore, just north of the town. This provided the cover he needed. A mile or so from the road to Achray he had chosen a site to build a bothy.

When he took his nephew, Willie MacGillivary, and one of his cattle herds, John Elrick, to show them the site just below a small wood at the foot of a cliff, they were most confused.

" There's no water here at all, uncle. How can we build a bothy here?" asked Willie. Elrick was silent. He had worked for MacFarlane for several years and knew he would have some trick worked out.

" Well Willie," said his uncle, " that's the whole point, don't you see? We're a bit close to the town and these damned Rangers from the Excise have been too active around here recently. So we build our bothy where there's no water"

" I don't understand at all. How can we make the stuff without water?" asked the young lad again. Just out of his teens, a stocky lad, taller and not as broad as his uncle but with the same red hair, Willie was keen to get started but was beginning to think his canny and successful uncle was not in full command of his senses.

" Well, what do you think then, John?" Macfarlane asked Elrick.

69

Tales of Whisky and Smuggling

" Och well, it would be hard to see the smoke against the trees there, and I suppose if there's no water here now, then maybe we could bring it in," replied the cattle herd.

" Aye that's right John, you've got it," smiled MacFarlane. " Look up there Willie," he said pointing up to the shoulder of Craigmore that jutted out above them, the top of which was almost a mile away. " Just up there there's a burn which runs down through the next wee glen. If we dug a ditch down past here and down there," again he pointed, this time down the hill to where a burn could be seen half a mile down the slope, " the water would come by just as nice as you like"

" But that would be just like another burn." protested young MacGiilivary.

" The Rangers would spot that , wouldn't they?"

" Not if we covered it over with stones and heather," laughed his uncle. " What do you think then Elrick?"

" It'll be a lot of work, but if we hide the bothy right, nobody'll ever guess it is there. We will have to be careful coming in and out though." Elrick said musingly.

." Aye, it'll be a bit of work, but if we came up with a couple of the other lads one or two Sundays I'm sure we could manage it no bother at all," MacFarlane stated with enthusiasm. " Then we could build the bothy at our leisure and pretty soon we'll have as nice a wee still going as you would like. The ditch will bring the clear water in and take away all our waste down to that other burn. I've given this a lot of thought and I don't think the Rangers will ever find it at all. "

As soon as he clearly understood what his uncle had in mind, Young Willie became enthusiastic and wanted to start right away. MacFarlane had been planning this for a while, however, and insisted that everything be done according to plan. Within a few weeks, the digging and covering over of the ditch having taken quite a bit more work than MacFarlane had first thought, the sma' still was turning out top quality peatreek, tended mainly by Willie and Elrick.

Travelling all over the country in his cattle-dealing business MacFarlane began to develop quite a sideline in the peatreek and added another still in the bothy on Craigmore. Though the extra income was appreciated he was in truth, more concerned with making and drinking his peatreek than with selling it. But he was delighted with the success of the venture and toyed with the idea of building some more stills. He could distribute the whisky under cover of his cattle-dealing business. However, though he let trusted friends in various locations have the odd flagon, and though the wee business showed a fair profit, he was busy enough with his legitimate business and didn't have the time, or the need, to expand his peatreek enterprise further.

Willie though, soon became a full-time smuggler, usually helped by John Elrick, though sometimes MacFarlane or one of his other men would give him a hand instead. He was always very careful to check he wasn't being followed and varied his route in and out of the bothy all the time. MacFarlane's peatreek soon became sought after in the Aberfoyle area, which gave the cattle-dealer a great deal of satisfaction - a satisfaction only surpassed when he took a dram or two himself of an evening. Being a successful businessman he moved in respectable company and many of the local gentry developed a taste for his *poit dubh* when they called at his home for an evening of cards. He regularly played cards with the local doctor and other businessmen in the evenings. Their favourite game was whist and over the course of such evenings a fair amount of peatreek was generally consumed.

This situation carried on for a few years and MacFarlane continued to thrive in the cattle business - his habit of sealing a bargain by bringing out a small flagon his own whisky ensuring many a convivial and advantageous business arrangement. Although everything was running smoothly MacFarlane continued to insist that everyone involved remained aware of the danger from the gaugers and that care was always taken to cover their tracks.

However it wasn't carelessness that proved the undoing of MacFarlane's wee business.

The authorities had become disturbed by the blatant behaviour of large convoys of smugglers who were coming from Lochtayside round through Glenfinglas, past the Brig o' Turk and through Aberfoyle before heading further south to Glasgow. Several Rangers were out looking to interrupt these arrogant Highland smugglers. One of them was a man who had been sent up from the South of England where he had been successful against the contraband trade. His name was Shortus. He was a wiry, powerful man of medium height in his late thirties, with greying hair and piercing blue eyes. As many smugglers in the South could testify, he was also a determined, pugnacious and aggressive character. The roving commission to find out as much as he could about the Lochtayside smugglers suited him well. Working on his own, he had been getting used to the wild and beautiful hills between Glasgow and Killin. Though it was totally different from the countryside he was used, to he adapted well and began to enjoy his sojourns in the hills.

Early one autumn morning, he was out on the slopes of Craigmore, spyglass in hand, looking north for signs of a rumoured convoy. He had spent the night on the hill having expected the convoy the previous evening.

Tales of Whisky and Smuggling

When night fell he had wrapped himself in a blanket and slept out among the heather. It was a beautiful morning and he was about to look towards Glenfinglas when, out of the corner of his eye, he saw a movement, below him to his right. At once he kneeled down, raised his spyglass and swung it round to watch the distant figure. The man below him looked round several times as he went into a hollow at the end of which was a cliff face with a small wood at its foot. Intrigued, he continued to watch. Just below the wood, the figure suddenly disappeared among the heather.

" Aha! " Shortus thought. " Another of these damned smugglers. Now where has he gone."

He continued to watch, and after a few minutes, a tell-tale column of smoke began to rise. No doubt about it, there was a distilling bothy down there. Although there was only one smuggler, he decided against approaching him directly. That way he might get the smuggler, but if the man put up much of a fight he might get away and he would only get the still. He wanted to destroy the still *and* arrest the man. He was also beginning to realise that he was hungry, very hungry. The bread and cheese he had brought in his bag had been finished the previous night. Decisive as ever, he made a careful note of where the still lay and headed down the hill away from the still, towards Aberfoyle.

Soon afterwards Shortus presented himself to the Supervisor of Excise in Aberfoyle. It didn't take the pair of them long to decide that this was probably MacFarlane's still. The Supervisor had long suspected its existence, but all his efforts at finding its location had proved fruitless.

"James MacFarlane eh? Is he well known blackguard then?" he demanded of the Supervisor, Peter Lilburn.

" Actually, he's a well respected man of business in the town. He deals mainly in cattle," replied Lilburn.

" What?" Shortus almost shouted. " If he has been making illicit spirits he is a common criminal and I shall bring this well respected gentleman to book."

"Yes, yes, of course you are right. I'll get a couple of men right away." spluttered the Supervisor, a bit taken aback at Shortus' vehemence.

" Never mind,' replied Shortus. " It's not yet lunch time. I will have something to eat and I will go back alone and arrest this man of business." He had no intention of letting anyone else know what was happening, certain that word would quickly pass around the community if they told Lilburn's men. It was better to trust no one.

" I'll thank you Supervisor if you will tell no-one at all. I can handle this myself. If I have not returned by five o'clock you and some of your local men can come after me," Shortus said stiffly.

A Tragic Feud

He gave Lilburn the location of the still, stressing the continuing need for secrecy. He then ate at a local inn, went into a shop to buy a couple of items and headed back up towards the still.

As he approached the still he pulled out his spyglass and directed it at the small wood at the bottom of the hill. There, sitting outside the still, was a stocky red-headed figure. It was Willie, taking a breather, and a dram, just outside the well concealed bothy. Due to his uncle's constant stressing of the need for caution, Willie had developed the habit of regularly looking around all the approaches to the still. He too had a telescope and he raised it to sweep over the rise below him.

"What is that?" he said to himself as he moved the telescope back. There was a man looking directly at him through another spy-glass. Dressed like that he was no local. Damn it: he was probably a gauger. Willie thought briefly of facing up to the man who was now walking directly up the hill towards him and the still. He could handle any government lackey. Then he remembered what his uncle had said.

" If by some chance the gaugers do find the still, just get away, I dont want any fuss, do you hear? We can always build another still but I dont want to be up in court. It could damage my business. Just run off into the heather if the gaugers come."

As Shortus approached, the figure disappeared into the bothy for a few moments, re-appearing with a sack and a flagon, then ran off up the hill.

" Run if you like, MacFarlane," Shortus yelled. " I will see you in court very soon."

Taking his time, he came to where he had seen the man duck into the bothy. Even close up he would never have seen it without the tell-tale wisps of smoke from the fire Willie had doused before running off. Methodically, Shortus smashed up the stills with the hammer and chisel he had bought in Aberfoyle, leaving the worms intact to take with him a proof.

He was back in the village well before five o'clock and went again to the Supervisor's Office to swear out a warrant against James MacFarlane. He was not aware that MacFarlane himself was in Glasgow on business that day.

When he received the summons, James MacFarlane laughed. It was not a pleasant laugh. He had been upset to lose his bothy and its two stills, but he appreciated that it was not Willie's fault.

" Och well," he said. " I have witnesses to say I was in Glasgow. This wee English gauger will not convict me."

The day of the trial came at the court in Callander. The courtroom was full, many of James' friends having come to see him put one over on this bumptious English gauger.

James' turn came. Shortus had stated that he had seen James MacFarlane run off from the bothy. Almost everyone in the courtroom knew that it was Willie who had run off. Sure they looked alike but James had a witness there from Glasgow. Carefully James answered all questions put to him. Then Willaim Sinclair, a butcher from Glasgow gave his evidence. He had been with James MacFarlane that day in Glasgow. So there was no way he could have been on the slopes of Craigmore.

Shortus was recalled and the magistrate said, " Officer Shortus, you have heard this witness. Are you still sure that it was James MacFarlane you saw run from the stillhouse on Craigmore?"

" Yes sir, I am certain. I know that it was him. He is a smuggler, " the gauger was adamant. In this situation the magistrate had little choice. The revenue man would not admit a mistake. James was found guilty. In fact his witness counted against him. He had tried to escape the law.

"James MacFarlane," the magistrate told him, " it is only your previous good character that stops you from going to jail. Fined thirty pounds."

The people in the courtroom gasped. James was stunned. He sat stony-faced. This was a swingeing fine indeed but that was of little matter. He had been in Glasgow and this gauger upstart had denied his word in open court. As he left the court, James glared at Shortus and said to John Elrick, " I'll take the worth of that £30 out of his English hide."

He could lose the still, another could be built. He could pay the fine. It was a great deal of money but he could raise it. What he could not overturn and what offended every ounce of his being was that he had been unjustly branded a liar. Shortus had no idea of what he had done. To him, these Highland smugglers were little more than savages. Even MacFarlane with his front of being a successful man of business, was just a savage at heart - and not for a moment did he doubt that it was MacFarlane he had seen that day on the hill.

MacFarlane was of Highland descent and like all Highlanders what mattered most to him was his sense of honour. Sure he could cheat the government of its revenue, but making whisky was his ancient right. He could even accept that if caught breaking the law he should be fined - that had nothing to do with honour. But to be branded a liar in open court, that was unforgiveable, and he would have his revenge.

A few months passed and MacFarlane seemed to have calmed down. He was travelling round the country on business as usual. However, as he travelled he kept an eye open for Shortus. The Revenue man travelled regularly through the Arerfoyle area and soon MacFarlane had a fair idea of his movements. He had not forgotten nor forgiven - he would have his revenge.

At last his chance came. He had seen Shortus in Aberfoyle. The Ranger had come from the south, stopping off to see Supervisor Lilburn. It was late afternoon in March when Shortus left Aberfoyle on the road to the Trossachs. He had not ridden far when he saw a heavily wrapped rider approaching. Thinking nothing of it he rode on. As they passed the other rider lashed out with a cudgel he had been holding behind his back . Shortus fell from his horse. The other dismounted quickly. Struggling to his feet the Englishman received another blow and then another, collapsing under the attack. The figure standing over him pulled the scarf from his face and threw off his hat. It was MacFarlane. Perhaps the gauger said something wrong, which further incensed the cattle-dealer, or perhaps it was MacFarlane's intention all the time. Whatever the reason, the gauger had no chance to defend himself and by the time his assailant remounted, he had been battered into an unconsciousness from which he would never rouse.

MacFarlane had laid his plans well. He rode off towards a friend's house just north of Aberfoyle, leaving the road and circling through the heather to approach the house from the south. It was the house of Doctor Meiklejohn, where MacFarlane and others regularly came to play cards and sip at the peatreek till well into the night. The bloodstained cudgel was thrown among the heather.

They had played only a couple of hands of cards when there was a thunderous hammering upon the doctor's door. There stood Moodie the local miller. " Quick, quick, Doctor. There's a very badly hurt man up the road a bit," he said breathlessly .

Grabbing his bag, Meiklejohn quickly saddled his horse and headed up the road with the miller, followed by MacFarlane and the others. Soon they came upon the still form of Shortus.

" My God, it's that gauger Shortus," exclaimed the doctor,'" someone has given him a terrible beating."

At once, with MacFarlane's willing assistance, they put the almost lifeless Englishman across one of the horses and took him back to Meiklejohn's house. It was soon obvious that despite the doctor's skill Shortus was dying. Within a few hours he died. In the meantime MacFarlane and one of his companions had gone to report the matter to the sheriff at Callander.

No one could be found who had seen anything and it was assumed that the abrasive gauger had been waylaid by some of the smugglers from Lochtayside whom everyone knew he was after. MacFarlane had played the good Samaritan well and no suspicion ever fell on him.

The only person who ever thought, even briefly that the cattle-dealer might have been involved was Willie MacGillivary. He had been surprised when he asked his uncle," Now someone's put an end to that Shortus man, will we building another bothy?"

Tales of Whisky and Smuggling

" No. I have no wish to return to that business, Willie. But if you wish I will set you up in a bothy - as long as it's not around here. I am a respectable cattle-dealer and wish to have no more involvement in the smuggling business," his uncle replied.

Willie wondered about that for a while but with a brand new bothy in the hills above Callander to tend, and peatreek to distribute to a ready list of customers, he soon let it pass. James MacFarlane continued to supply his card-playing friends with whisky he bought from his nephew, but never again did he think of making the peatreek.

Arran of the Many Kegs

As far back as the eighth century and before, the Celtic bards sang the praises of the Isle of Arran. Set in the middle of the Firth of Clyde this beautiful island ranges from the fertile lands of Kilmory and Bennan on the southern coast to the wild and rugged mountains of Goat Fell, Benn Tarsuinn and Benn Bharrain in the north. This was the favourite hunting ground of Celtic Kings and heroes from Alba and Erin (Scotland and Ireland), heroes like Finn MacCoul and his warrior band the *Fianna* or Fenians, the tales of whom were told throughout Ireland and Scotland wherever Gaelic was spoken. Nowadays Arran is just as popular with the crowds who come over on the ferry from Ayrshire and Glasgow on every public holiday. Though the eastern coast is heavily developed to cater for day-trippers and other tourists, the west coast overlooking the Kilbrandon sound and the Mull of Kintyre is quieter and is in many ways like the Hebrides with the advantage of the Mull keeping off much of the Atlantic wind. With its ancient standing stones, its chambered cairns and the brooding, enigmatic stone circles of Machrie Moor, the island has a feel of never having let go of its past.

And in the heyday of the smuggling Arran had its place. Just a few miles over the Firth of Clyde lay the then busy seaports of the Ayrshire coast and beyond them lay the great city of Glasgow, always welcoming the contents of the sma' stills. Although the Gaelic language was fading in Arran by the early nineteenth century, a process much speeded up by some wholesale clearances of entire glens, there were traditions of the Gael that survived. One of these of course was the making of the peatreek. The geography of the island greatly helped. Apart from a narrow coastal strip round much of the island and the area around Machrie Moor, all of Arran is Highland terrain from the 1500 feet of Tighvein in the south to the great massif of mountains spreading from the 2868 feet high Goat Fell in the north. There are a host of

Tales of Whisky and Smuggling

small glens with fast-flowing burns which provided perfect locations for the smugglers' trade.

However in Arran they didn't just have gaugers to contend with. To stop the ferrying over of whisky from Kintyre and Arran there was a revenue cutter, seconded from the Royal Navy which constantly patrolled the Firth.

In the years between 1810 and 1820 the struggle between the smugglers and the revenue men intensified. Pressure from the large-scale manufacturers of spirits, mainly in the south of England and the state of war with Napoleonic France made the situation worse. There were riots in Stirling, Kilmarnock, Aberdeenshire and elsewhere in some of which smugglers were killed. Arran was no exception. The heavy hand of government coming up against the often bloody-minded independence of the Gael guaranteed such conflict.

In March 1817, John McKinnon of Kildonan in the south of Arran, and his son, also John, had a cargo of peatreek ready to be transported over the Firth of Clyde to a contact in the seaside town of Saltcoats. Some of the whisky they had made themselves in their bothy in the foothills of Tighvein and the rest of it had been made by friends and neighbours. At this time of year the weather was rarely settled and this worried them. With the vigour and enthusiasm of his youth, twenty year old Young John urged his father to cross by night. " The cutter'll never catch us if we go in the dark father, " he pleaded. " The weather's not been too bad. We can do it."

" No, no, I don't think we should try it at all," said his father. "Remember what happened last November. Sandy Campbell and both his brothers went down trying to cross at night. That was a sore loss to their family that."
" Och father that was in November. We're into the Spring now." his son went on. " The weather's nowhere near so bad."

" No I've made up my mind," his father stated firmly. " We'll set off at first light. Nobody has seen the cutter since last week. It could be up watching the Bute men. We'll go in the morning."

They proceeded to load the whisky that night and grabbed a few hours sleep. As dawn began to lighten the sky, the wee fishing dinghy put out from a bay above Kildonan. The weather was calm with hardly a breath of wind. The two McKinnons were rowing steadily and powerfully out from the shelter of the island when a long sleek shape appeared from the mainland side of Holy Island. It was the revenue cutter Prince Edward. The watch on the cutter were wide awake and had seen the small craft put out. At first the father and son didn't see the cutter coming down from the north. It came closer and closer. Suddenly Young John saw it.

" Father, turn about. It's the cutter," he shouted.

Immediately they turned the small boat - a manoeuvre that let the Prince Edward gain a little more on them. It was now less than a mile away. With many more oarsmen handling its great sweeps, the cutter was much faster than the little fishing boat and as the morning breezes gathered the sail was hoisted. Straining furiously the McKinnons forced their boat through the water. Not a word was spoken. All their efforts were concentrated on reaching the shore before the cutter caught up with them.

By now the chase had been spotted on shore and word quickly spread. There was no way of getting back to Kildonan before the cutter caught up, so the small boat veered quickly and headed directly to the shore just north of Largybeg. As they approached the beach a crowd had gathered. The local people needed no-one to tell them what was happening out on the water. There was no hesitation. The crowd had gathered to help unload and scatter the peatreek. Everybody in that crowd was ready to flout the law in the case of whisky. They would do their damndest to keep the barrels of whisky out of the hands of the revenue men and the navy.

The cutter continued to close on the smaller boat. From the Prince Edward the mate, John Jeffrey, who was in temporary command of the vessel, called out, " Heave to in the name of the King."

The McKinnons ignored him and pressed on. The cutter closed further. The dinghy grounded on the beach. Out leapt McKinnon and his son and they began unloading the ankers of peatreek. From the cutter a long boat was lowered and within minutes armed gaugers were running towards the smaller boat. Down the beach streamed a crowd of locals. The gaugers reached the McKinnons with Jeffrey, sword in hand, in the lead. At once several of the barrels were seized. The elder McKinnon tried to resist Jeffrey and was struck down. The local people kept coming. Barrels were torn from the gaugers' hands. Fists, sticks and then swords began to fly. Seeing his father fall young John siezed a gaff from the dinghy and lunged at Jeffrey. A shot rang out, then another and another. Bodies fell. The locals hesitated. "Form a line men," cried Jeffrey, as more men came from the Prince Edward, firearms in hand.

" Desist in the name of the King," called Jeffrey as the gaugers and sailors from the Prince Edward aimed their pieces at the crowd. The crowd fell back, dragging several wounded. There on the beach between the government men and the natives were the barrels of peatreek and three still bodies.

" You are all under arrest," shouted Jeffrey. Looking at the bodies and the levelled guns, the Arran people made a decision. Almost as one they turned and fled. They would fight against swords but to go against the firepower before them would be madness.

Tales of Whisky and Smuggling

" Stay where you are," screamed Jeffrey, " Stop or we fire."

Behind him, the gaugers and Marines looked at each other. Shooting in the heat of battle was one thing - they had been under attack - but none of them was going to shoot people in the back. Despite Jeffrey's yells the crowd melted away.

Stepping forward the mate of the Prince Edward turned over the bodies, one of them a woman. Both the McKinnons and Isobel Nicholl, a wife and mother from Largybeg, were dead.

" Damned smugglers," Jeffrey spat out. " Right men load the whisky on the cutter and let's be away. I don't like the look of that crowd."

Soon the disputed peatreek was loaded and the cutter was rowed out into the bay and sailed away, leaving the three bodies on the beach.

There was uproar throughout Arran and on the mainland when the news broke. The killing of the McKinnons was bad enough, but killing a woman was truly shocking. Also two of the wounded in the crowd on the beach had been children. Public opinion demanded something be done. The government realised they could not just let the incident pass. So Jeffrey was charged with assault and various other charges. The people wanted him charged with murder but thought that anything was better than nothing. There were two grieving families who attended Jeffrey's trial six months later, in Glasgow. They knew their loved ones had broken the law, but they were there to see justice done. Surely they had not deserved to be slaughtered for smuggling and trying to get away from the revenue.

The Government had let the immediate furore die down and the verdict against Jeffrey was Not Guilty on all charges. However, because of the depth of feeling against him on Arran, Jeffrey was sent elsewhere.

The revenue men did not always win on Arran. A few months after Jeffrey's trial the gaugers had located a still at Ballymichael near Shiskine in the west of Arran. They had caught Paul Campbell in the act of making whisky. Campbell was a hot-headed young man, short, stocky, as dark as a gypsy and known to be a bit of a wild man. When three gaugers arrived at his still, he had not hesitated and had attacked them. He felled one outright then, taking a few blows himself, managed to push the others off. He took off through the heather but the gaugers caught up with him and after a short bloody fight his hands were tied and he was taken to Brodick. The first gauger he had hit was quite badly hurt and it was decided to send the smuggler to Glasgow to stand trial for assault of a revenue officer.

A few days later, Campbell was put on board the ship Islay, the captain of which was John MacArthur, like Campbell, a Gaelic-speaker. Once on board ship the two gaugers accompanying Campbell relaxed. There was no way

Campbell could get away from them on board ship - or so they thought. Campbell's hands were handcuffed before him and they let him roam free around the ship.

" Enjoy it while you can, Campbell," said gauger Wilson. " You'll be seeing nothing but prison walls for the rest of your life." His companion laughed at this, but all Campbell did was look long and hard at them. In truth his situation looked hopeless. Why hadn't he gone with his brother Martin? He had gone off to America and had written Paul a letter saying he was doing well for himself near a place called New Orleans and why didn't Paul come and join him? Ruefully, Paul looked around the Firth of Clyde at the beautiful islands and mountains on his left - sights he would probably never see again. He was standing gazing hopelessly over at the island of Bute when he heard someome approach him. It was John MacArthur. Placing his hand on Campbell's shoulder the sailor let out a short burst of Gaelic, waited for Campbell's nod and hurried away. No-one had noticed. There was something immediately different about Campbell. He was standing much straighter and a glint had come into his eye.

A few hours later the Islay had passed by Greenock and was heading up the ever-narrowing river. Closer and closer to the south bank of the river the ship sailed. It was only a few dozen yards from the shore when Campbell made his move. He climbed up on the rail. Pausing only to shout something in Gaelic, he dived over. The splash alerted Wilson and looking over the ship's side, he saw Campbell in the water. Even with his handcuffs he was swimming powerfully through the water.

"Stop the boat, stop at once! " cried Wilson.

Seeing what was happening, his companion, Christie, ran to the captain and roared, " In the King's name stop the boat. Our prisoner has jumped overboard. Stop at once I say."

" Och I'm sorry Officer, indeed I am but there's bad currents about here and I would endanger my ship if I stopped. You'll just have to wait a bit," MacArthur calmly replied. Christie, cursing with frustration, ran back to join Wilson at the ship's starboard rail. There in the distance they could just see Campbell pulling himself out on to the bank. Standing up he gave the gaugers a double-handed wave, called out something in Gaelic and ran off. That was the last they saw of him.

Having sold his peatreek in the area, Campbell had friends along the banks of the Clyde and soon a friendly blacksmith had him free of his handcuffs. Within weeks he had gathered enough money for his fare to America and soon left from Liverpool to join his brother. MacArthur wasn't even suspected - the gaugers had not understood the thanks and blessing their prisoner had called to the captain. Being fond of a dram of peatreek

Tales of Whisky and Smuggling

himself, MacArthur had been incensed by the happenings at Largybeg and saw helping Campbell as his contribution to helping square accounts with the government.

The people of Largybeg of course were unlikely to forget the fate of Isobel Nicholl and the McKinnons. One of those who had been involved in the battle on the beach was Dan Cook. His croft was on the seashore not far from the fateful beach and he had his still on the hillside not far to the north. Like his neighbours his hatred for the Excisemen was total after what had happened and like them he was much more careful than before in his activities. One day he had brought back the worm of his still and other bits and pieces to his house. He was going to look closely at them as he hadn't been too happy with his last batch of whisky. He wasn't sure what was wrong but checking over the equipment at his leisure would do no harm.

Suddenly he heard a noise. Looking out of his door he saw a longboat from the Prince Edward landing between him and the location of his still. He would never get to the still before them. There were several flagons of his last batch still there, as well as the rest of his equipment. Suddenly he became aware that a couple of the gaugers were heading towards his house, cutlasses in hand. He was alone as his wife had gone into the village and his sons were off fishing. As the gaugers approached the house they split up. These weren't green young lads, they knew what they were about. One came to the front door, the other to the back. In the distance the larger party was heading off up into the hills.

Moments later the gauger at the front of the house shouted, " Right in we go."

Both doors were opened at the same time. Inside the house all was dark. All each gauger could see was a pitchfork aimed directly at his face. Not a sound could be heard. In the dark in the middle of the small croft house Dan Cook was standing holding two pitchforks tied together by the handles. It appeared to the gaugers that each was facing a dangerously armed man.

The one at the front of the house shouted. " Off you go and get some more men. I'll keep an eye on these two."

Off ran the gauger. As soon as he had gone Dan Cook lunged at the other. The man backed off and Dan ran at him. Going backwards the gauger tripped over his heels. His cutlass flew from his hand. In an instant Dan was on him and stunned him with a heavy blow from his fist. At that point his wife Catriona came hurrying up. Grabbing a sack from an outhouse, she slipped it over the gauger's head. In a matter of minutes they had the revenue man trussed up and stuck him in the peatstack just south of the house.

"Quickly now, let's get the gear in the house down to the cave," Dan said quietly, moving quickly towards the house. It was a matter of only a few more minutes before the equipment and two big-bellied bottles of whisky were taken down to the beach and hidden in a small cave in the rocks above the beach. Pushing the boulder that covered the entrance to the cave back into place, Dan rubbed his hands together.

" Right Catriona, let's back to the house and we'll just tell the others when they arrive that we have no idea at all what happened to that poor man in our peat stack" he said.

" And what man is there in our peat stack, husband?" retorted his wife, laughing.

By the time the other gauger returned with three others, all carrying guns, Dan was standing calmly at his front door, watching them approach.

As they came close the three armed men pointed their weapons at the big crofter.

" Och fire away,' called Dan contemptuously, wiping his nose with the back of his hand. " You've had plenty practice shooting unarmed women and children. "

Taken aback the gaugers said nothing.

" Oh is it a different thing to be shooting at men then?" Dan added.

The men looked shamefaced, but the guns remained pointing at Cook. At last the gauger who had gone for help angrily demanded, " Where is the officer I left here a quarter of an hour ago?"

" A quarter of an hour ago is it? " said Dan innocently. " Why my wife and I have just returned a minute ago from Largybeg." He turned and called into the house, " Catriona there's a man from the Excise here asking if we have seen one of his fellows hereabouts."

At that Catriona came to the door. " A gauger? No we haven't seen any one at all. We' re just back to the house from Largybeg. You will be knowing where that is will you not?" she added, having heard every word Dan had said.

" Search the buildings." the gauger blurted to his fellows, taking one of the guns and pointing it at Dan. " He's here somewhere." The pointed remarks about the recent killings were making him feel uncomfortable.

They soon located the gauger tied up in the peat stack. He was still dazed and seemed not to know where he was.

" Right you blackguard, we have you now," crowed his friend.

" I have never seen this fellow before. Have you Catriona?" Dan asked innocently.

" No, I don't think I know him at all. I wonder how he came to be in our peatstack. As we said, Officer we have been down in the village. You can ask

Tales of Whisky and Smuggling

anybody down there at all," Catriona smiled sweetly.

" Do you think he could have tied himself up?" Dan asked smiling.

The gaugers were furious but as they untied their companion it was obvious he was totally confused. Things had happened so fast that he couldn't be sure who had attacked him. He had certainly not seen Catriona and was too dazed still to do as his companion clearly wanted and identify Dan as his assailant.

At that point the Lieutenant in charge of the Prince Edward came up. Listening carefully to what his men said, he looked long and hard at Dan, who smiled gently back. There were two of them and no witness against them but the dazed gauger. Lieutenant Smythe was a gentleman and he would not stoop to lying just to help the Revenue gain a conviction. Though shaken, the gauger they had found in the peatstack seemed not to be badly hurt. So the small group of government men headed off to join the others in their search of the area. They located Dan's still and sadly, two others, but as Dan had his worm safely hidden away it wasn't long before he had built a new bothy in another spot and was producing peatreek again.

Over on the Mull of Kintyre relations between smugglers and gaugers were not as bad. As in so many other locations, there was what can almost be described as a working relationship between them. The gaugers knew their livelihood depended on there being smugglers and the smugglers knew that if they kept the gaugers "sweet" their lives would be much easier. This lead to many of the gaugers and smugglers being on almost friendly terms.

One fine summer's day Andrew MacInnes, a notorious long-term smuggler, was at his favourite occupation at his still. This was located by a hilltop spring very close to the cliffs near Achinhoan Head opposite Arran. He had not heard that there were any gaugers in the area so wasn't being particularly careful. However a pair of gaugers, Messrs Nicoll and Patterson had come over from Campbelltown and had seen the smoke from Andrew's fire. They left their horses a bit away and crept quietly up to the top of the hill, where Andrew was singing away happily to himself as he tended his still.

" Got you Andrew MacInnes," shouted Nicoll as the gaugers jumped out of the trees surrounding Andrew's chosen spot.

" Aye we have you this time Andrew," added Patterson. " You'd better put out that fire."

" Och right enough you've got me this time," said Andrew ruefully, his mind racing.

" Aye that we have," continued Nicoll. " We'll take the still once you've emptied it all out."

Seeing there was little to be done, MacInnes doused his fire and as soon as it was cool enough he emptied out the various pieces of his still and piled them up ready for the gaugers to take away. When this was all done, the gaugers sitting on the grass watching him dismantle the still, he said, " Look lads, I've had a hard time of it lately and I could do without the fine."

" What are you suggesting MacInnes? Are you trying to bribe us?" demanded Patterson.

" No, no not at all. I was just thinking... it's a fine warm day, not a day to be carrying all this stuff all the way back to Campbelltown. I could save you all that bother, and the bother of taking me to court, if I just threw the whole lot of this old still over the cliff and into the sea here. It's nearly worn out anyway," Andrew said mildly.

The gaugers looked at each other. It was an old still and not worth much to them. They hadn't confiscated any whisky to auction off. And if Andrew's still went into the Kilbrandon Sound they could truthfully claim to their Supervisor that they had put one smuggler out of business.

They couldn't see any flaw at all in Andrew's suggestion so agreed and happily watched as the smuggler threw his beloved old still over the cliff top with many a sigh and expression of regret.

When it was all gone, MacInnes put out his hand to Nicoll. " Just to say there's no hard feelings gentlemen, though I have had that still for a good long time you know, " he said, looking a bit downcast.

" Aye fair enough," said Nicoll, as he, then Patterson shook the elderly MacInnes by the hand then left to go to their horses and ride on their way.

As he watched them go Andrew MacInnes shook his head slowly from side to side. Looking up at the sun and doing a quick calculation, he headed for his home at Kilddalloig.

Several hours later he was back in the area. This time he was on the beach below the cliff. There on the beach at the foot of the cliff were the various pieces of his beloved old still. He had correctly figured that the ebbing tide wouldn't move them far. The tun and the flakestand were a little scratched and dented but two days later Andrew was singing to himself as he got another batch of peatreek under way - from now on he would be sure to tend his still in the night time - even the gaugers wouldn't fall for the same trick twice!

In The Shadow of Schiehallion

Between Loch Tay and Loch Rannoch stands the beautiful mountain of Schiehallion. Its name in Gaelic means the Fairy Hill of the Caledonians. Since the long distant times when the Caledonian tribes fought the Romans, and stopped them conquering what is now Scotland, this mountain has had a special place in the heart of the Gael. Many tales were told of the Fairy Hill and in the days of the peatreek there was a great deal of activity round and about its foothills. Like their neighbours on Lochtayside to the south of Schiehallion, the people of Loch Rannoch and Loch Tummel were dedicated to making their own whisky. And like their neighbours they too were highly inventive in thwarting the gaugers who tried so hard to limit if not stamp out the peatreek industry.

The beautiful and rugged glens of Highland Perthshire supplied the *uisge beatha* to willing customers as far away as Dundee and Glasgow and there are tales suggesting their produce was appreciated over the border in England. In these Highland glens the gaugers always had a hard time. The close-knit, Gaelic-speaking communities were totally foreign to the usually Lowland-born gaugers. Adding to the problem was the fact that most of the local people remembered stories of the government brutality after the great tragedy of Culloden. Less than a hundred years had passed since Butcher Cumberland's troops had pillaged and slaughtered their way through the Highlands after that day on Drumossie Moor, and the Gaels have always had long memories. Stories were still told of the famous Cateran, Sergeant Mor whose band of cattle-raiders had lived as outlaws for several years after Culloden, gathering annually on Rannoch Moor with other bands, as many as 400 men in all. No wonder then that the gaugers so often felt the whole country was against them, as in truth it was.

There was little in fact that gave the Highlanders more pleasure than outwitting the gaugers. If, however, brute force was needed to convey their wares to their waiting thirsty customers, they had no objection to that either. Highland Perthshire was a rough posting for the gaugers and they very rarely went about their business alone.

One day a band of four gaugers was riding slowly along the road to Kinloch Rannoch. The sun was glinting off the murmuring River Tummel through the trees on their left as they rode along, enjoying the clear autumn day. The leaves on the trees were a glorious mix of golds, russets and browns and the birds were singing. It was hardly a day to be thinking about catching smugglers and the gaugers were relaxed and enjoying the peaceful day as they rode along.

Just as they were passing by the farm of Tomanbuidhe they saw a cart coming towards them. It was being led by two strapping young men and the cart looked to be piled high with straw. As the cart approached the leading gauger held up his hand and called out, " Halt in the King's name."

The cart halted and the four gaugers rode up to it. There on the straw was a feeble-looking old man, covered with a ragged blanket, his eyes closed and breathing heavily through his gaping mouth.

" Who is he and what is wrong with him," the leading gauger asked.

" Och that is our old grandfather sir, and we are thinking that he has the *leisg dubh* on him," the taller of the two young men, Donald Robertson replied.

The gaugers backed their horses off a bit. Whatever this was it sounded ominous. A couple of them recognised the word *dubh*, meaning black, and this reassured them not at all.

" Is it catching?" the gauger went on, showing a reluctance to dismount and look closer at the old man who, at that moment gave out a sound between a grunt and a groan. The gaugers looked at each other and backed their mounts off another yard.

" Well, sir, as to that we are not sure, but it is incurable without a doubt. We have tried everything but the *leisg dubh* is still on him," Donald sadly said.

" Where are you taking him?" came another question.

"Well sir," this time it was Archie, the younger brother, who spoke,"there is an old man near Pitlochry that we think might be doing our grandfather a bit of good."

" Right, well, em, on you go, on you go," the gauger said, as the four horsemen drew back to let the cart and its passenger pass.

As the cart headed on towards Loch Tummel the gaugers urged their horses to a canter and were soon out of sight of the grinning Robertson brothers. As soon as they were out of sight their passenger sat up and burst out laughing. Underneath the straw were forty gallons of peatreek, destined to be carried further south by the man they were meeting at Pitlochry - truly the payment he would eventually bring them would make old Willie Robertson feel a lot better.

" *Ochone, ochone,* " he said between bursts of laughter, "That was a good one Donald. Incurable indeed, you cheeky devil."

Donald thought he had done pretty well with those ignorant gaugers, fancy them being frightened of catching the black laziness!

Because of the close family relationships inherited from the old clan system, the usual habit of helping and supporting the smugglers was even stronger the further into the Highlands one went. It could seem that everybody in an area was related either by blood or marriage and this made the gaugers' task all the more frustrating. The chances of finding informers was slim and the speed at which news of excisemen's actions could spread was fantastic. Even when they did have some success in the hills, the gaugers had usually a good distance to travel back to where their confiscated goods, or prisoners, would be safe. Because of this remarkable loyalty among the communities in the Highlands the smuggling did not die out as early as elsewhere and even near the end of the nineteenth century there was still a brisk peatreek trade, though much diminished as glen after glen lost its people to the cities or to the still bleeding haemorrhage of emigration.

Some of the gaugers were particularly adept at their business. One such was Allan Simpson, who had come to the Highland glens from Dundee. On more than one occasion he had located stills far up in the hills near the summer shielings. These were the areas where for centuries the clanfolk had taken their cattle and other beasts to graze in the summer months. Whole communities would move up to spend the long summer days high in the hills, leaving behind only enough people to tend the crops and gardens in the glen valleys. By the early nineteenth century this system was beginning to become less common but the shielings with their stone and turf built houses continued to provide good locations for smugglers. Simpson knew of this and had developed a method of locating such stills.

With one other companion, he would take enough food for several days, blankets to sleep in at night and head for the hilltops. From on high he could spot the smoke from bothies and come down upon them from above.

One day he and a companion called Thomson had spotted a still at the top of Glen Mor between Schiehallion and Carn Mairg to the south. Getting as close as they could, the gaugers examined the situation through their spyglasses. They could see that there were four men at a large, well hidden bothy by a fast-flowing burn near a group of old shieling houses. One of them was someone Simpson had had his eye on for a while.

This was a well-known local character called Ewan Fletcher. He was a bit of a braggart and had a high opinion of his own capabilities. This led him to have a low opinion of most other people, but he saved the worst of his sarcastic tongue for the gaugers. He had often passed disparaging comments on the gaugers, usually in Gaelic, whenever he came across any of the revenue men. This often caused much mirth among his companions. He was an argumentative and arrogant man, about thirty years old, and his features were reddened by indulgence in his own peatreek.

" There's no way we can take on the four of them," said Thomson as the two gaugers lay in the heather on the hillside above the group of smugglers, "especially with that vicious brute Fletcher there."

" Hm, you're right, but look over there to the left," replied Simpson.

Looking through his spyglass to the spot indicated, Thomson saw a couple of sturdy Highland garrions, or ponies, tethered on long ropes and grazing peacefully.

" I see them, but what of it?" asked the puzzled gauger.

" Well, by the looks if things they haven't got all of their whisky yet. They're probably on the last run or they wouldn't have brought the ponies. There'll be a fair amount ready to go now, but not quite enough. We'll just bide our time and maybe we'll get a chance to confiscate it," Simpson told him.

" If they go," replied Thomson dourly.

" We'll just have to wait and see," his companion replied.

As the afternoon wore on, the gaugers kept watching the activities below. Most of the time the men were in the bothy but at about four o'clock all four of them came out together. After talking for a few minutes, Fletcher and two others headed off down the hill. They had left behind a young lad, who looked to be in his late teens, to watch the still.

"Right," said Simpson. We'll give them an hour to be on their way, then we'll go and relieve that young lad of the stuff and take it on the ponies to the inn at Foss. We'll stop there, have something to eat and press on to Pitlochry."

An hour later the two gaugers came down from the hill. They were just about a hundred yards from the bothy when the young man came out. He looked up the hill and saw the gaugers approaching. He stood rooted to the spot with surprise.

" Hey, you stay where you are! " called Thomson.

At that the lad whirled around, dived into the bothy and a moment later ran out clutching a flagon and took off down the glen. Thomson was abou to give chase when Simpson suddenly shouted loudly, "Head him off men."

Without changing his headlong pace, the lad whirled to his left and began running up the side of Craig an Earra, obviously thinking there were more gaugers ahead of him.

" What was that for?' asked Thomson, puzzled.

Laughing, his companion replied, " By the time he realises that there's only the two of us, he'll be a good bit off and we'll be between him and the others.'

" Right," said Thomson admiringly, " that's a good trick. I'll remember that.'

" You do that," said the smiling Simpson. The two gaugers quickly set to work smashing up the still. When they had finished that, they loaded the whisky that was already made onto the ponies and, after setting fire to the carefully built bothy, set off towards Foss.

Despite a shower of rain as they came down they made good time and reached Foss, about nine miles away, in well under three hours. Having spent the night on the hills and had a hard day's work with only bread and cheese to eat and water to drink they were glad indeed to reach the inn at Foss, where they could have a hot meal and a tankard or two of ale. It was early evening, about seven o'clock and they still had a further eleven miles to Pitlochry. Simpson was sure they would be able to hire a horse and cart. They would put the whisky in the cart, tie the confiscated ponies to it and ride back to Pitlochry.

Reaching the simple inn they hitched the ponies directly in front of the door, where they could keep an eye on them. Soon they were sitting at a table having a hot meal. They were pleased with themselves and Thomson was full of admiration for Simpson's methods.

While they were sitting there, Alexander Stewart arrived at the inn. He was a successful local farmer and had met gauger Simpson on a few occasions in the past. He also happened to be married to a cousin of Fletcher, a fact of which the gauger was totally unaware. He recognised the ponies. Stopping to whisper a message to a boy sitting outside, Stewart went in to the inn. Once he had gone in, the boy got up, in no hurry, and sauntered off. Round the corner, he burst into a run and headed off westwards.

" Well, good evening Mr. Simpson," Stewart called out on entering the inn, and walked over to the table where the gaugers had just finished their meal.

" Hello there Mr Stewart. How are you?" replied the gauger, pleased to see the farmer who he clearly recalled was a staunch government supporter and as such opposed to the smuggling business.

" This is my colleague, Walter Thomson. Thomson this is Mr James Stewart, a good friend," he said.

" You'll have a dram gentlemen - of the legal kind. None of that illegal brew is on sale here," he offered, turning away to wink at the landlord. Drinks were poured and the three of them sat at the table.

The gaugers were pleased to accept. It would be after dark before they got to Pitlochry anyway, so what difference would a few minutes make. Soon they were telling Stewart of the day's success against the notorious Fletcher. Seeming mightily impressed, Stewart offered to get them a horse and cart. This arrangement suited the gaugers, so Stewart sent another boy who had appeared at the inn to go and fetch a horse and cart from a nearby friend. While the laddie went off on his errand Stewart bought the gaugers another couple of drinks. They were feeling pretty proud of themselves by now and were regaling the farmer with tales of past successes against the smugglers.

After a while, as the evening beginning to draw on, the cart arrived with Stewart's friend. Terms were agreed and the gaugers rose to put the whisky on the cart.

" Och never mind. My friend Robertson here will do that for you, eh Sandy?" laughed Stewart, winking at Robertson, " and we'll have a last wee drink before you go."

This seemed an eminently sensible arrangement and Robertson went outside. Standing out of sight with six other barrels of the same size and weight as those on the horses were Fletcher and two others. Inside, the gaugers were toasting the health of Mr. Alexander Stewart and were paying no attention to what was going on outside.

Quickly the switch was made, the new barrels put on the cart and the two horse loosely tied to the back of the cart. A few minutes later the now merry gaugers came out and with a profusion of thanks to Stewart and Robertson they mounted the cart and rode off as dusk was falling. Fletcher and his friends stepped round the corner of the inn as the cart disappeared down the road with the two gaugers now bursting into song.

There was great merriment that night at the Foss inn, especially when two Highland ponies came walking along the road a while later.

Poor Simpson's strategies had proved insufficient and the Supervisor at Pitlochry was furious when two of his gaugers woke him from his bed that night. They were still in high spirits, but those spirits soon sank when they found that the barrels contained nothing but pure Highland water. Soon after this incident Simpson applied for a transfer which was soon granted.

Not long after this the Foss inn was a the scene for the swansong of a successful smuggler who soon after turned his particular talents in another direction.

This was Donald Cameron, a native of Lochaber who had fallen in love with a local lass when passing through the area with some cattle a few years before. Donald was known for his great love of being in the hills and spent hours watching birds and animals in the wild. Lithely built, he was a strong healthy specimen in his mid-twenties, with brown eyes and black curly hair and was possessed of a true Highland independence of spirit. Sadly his romantic feelings towards the object of his adoration were not reciprocated.

However Donald liked living in the shadow of Schiehallion and stayed on after his rejection by the young lady in question. Having learned the trade in Lochaber, *Domhnull Dubh* (Dark Donald) soon became involved in the local peatreek industry. He was happy to spend days on end tending a still up in the hills. Though he was successful Donald always had a hankering to leave the peatreek. He had an intense dislike of the hot, smoky and smelly interior of the bothies, much preferring to be in the open air. However to make a living he had to stoke the fire and watch over the still in the smoke and heat - there was no choice.

The methods that gauger Simpson had used had been noticed and others began to follow his example. It was a group of three gaugers who had stayed out on the hill overnight that managed to locate the still that Donald Dubh was running in a bothy high up on Meall Tarneachan to the south of Foss. Though they saw the still, Donald saw them and made off before they got to him. There wasn't a gauger born who could catch Donald Cameron on the hills, even without a head start. Actually, he hadn't been intending to start a new batch of whisky for a day or two. The smoke the gaugers had seen was from a fire over which he had been cooking a pair of lovely brown trout he had tickled that morning. The gaugers were appreciative of the cooked breakfast, which went some way to making up for the lack of peatreek in the bothy. They decided to take the still to pieces and use it as evidence in court. They knew it was Donald's still and would summons him to appear on a charge of smuggling. With the still as evidence and three witnesses they were sure of their case.

So they carefully took the still to pieces and carried the equipment to Foss. This took them quite a while and, being autumn it was nearing dusk when they got to Foss. Going to the inn the eldest, a man named Collins who was tall, thin and sallow-looking, said to the landlord, William Stewart, " We require a room for the night. A room with a lock on the door."

They were aware of what had happened to Simpson and Thomson and were going to make sure that they didn't end up looking stupid. So they took the sma' still up to the room and locked it and themselves in. They had their dinner sent up to them and resolved to stay there until first light, when they would rise and head to Pitlochry.

They were totally unaware that Donald had followed them off the hill. It was a simple matter to find out where the gaugers were. Next door to the inn there was a cottage having a new roof put on. Noticing the planks piled up there, Donald had an idea. Smiling to himself, he looked up at the window of the room where the gaugers were. Then he went off to visit a friend until well after nightfall. Just before midnight Donald came back. There was still a light on downstairs in the inn. He knocked gently on a window . After a moment the window opened and Willie Stewart stuck his head out and whispered, " Who is there?"

" It is me Willie, Donald Dubh," he whispered back.

" Ah it's yourself, " the innkeeper said quietly. " Those gauger fellows have got your still upstairs in the room, you know."

" Aye, I know. Do you think they are all asleep yet?" Donald inquired.

" Och I was up a few minutes ago, and there was nothing but snoring going on in that room. Mind you it's not surprising, they had quite a few tankards of ale, " Stewart whispered.

"Thanks a lot, that's what I wanted to know. Now you just go to bed yourself, William, "the smuggler said smiling.

" What are you going to do?" the innkeeper asked, obviously intrigued.

" Never you mind. You'll see soon enough, good night Willie," Donald said over his shoulder as he moved away from the window.

Minutes later, a dark figure could be seen in the starlight moving from the cottage being repaired towards the inn. It was Donald and he was carrying a long plank. Gently he placed the plank against the inn wall. It reached to just below the bedroom window. Quickly and quietly he fetched three more planks of the same length and laid them beside the first one.

Like a cat, silent in the night, Donald climbed up the planks. Slowly, ever so slowly, he took out a small knife and prised open the window. As soon as the window was open he dropped silently into the room. There was soft glow from the peat fire giving just enough light for the next part of his plan. Two of the gaugers were asleep on the bed and the third was wrapped in a blanket on the floor. Stepping gingerly round the man on the floor, he gathered up the three pairs of shoes from around the small room and threw them out of the window.

Everything was ready. Now it was all a matter of speed and luck. With the window wide open, Donald swiftly gathered up as much of his still as he could hold, leaving the worm near the window. Then with a heave he threw the still out of the window. Clang! Batter! Clash! The noise as the metal parts hit the ground rang out like a bell. All three gaugers sprang awake, just in time to see Donald climb out of the window clutching the worm and the last pieces of his still.

" After him!" shouted Collins. " He's getting away, after him."

Collins rushed to the window while the other two scrambled about on the floor looking for their shoes. Down below him he could clearly see Donald gathering up the bits of his still. He wouldn't be able to go fast or far with that load.

" You've gone too far Cameron, stealing from the Government. I'll see you in jail for this,' the gauger roared.

Tales of Whisky and Smuggling

" You'll be needing evidence for that," Donald sang back cheekily, as he gathered up the last of his pieces and staggered away.

" He's taken our shoes," one of the other gaugers yelled. " He's taken our shoes the damned blackguard."

" Light the lantern you fool," Collins shouted. "Quickly you fools quickly." He could still hear the parts of the still clanking together as Donald made off but the sound was lessening all the time.

By the time the gaugers were organised enough to find and put on their shoes there was only the faintest noise of Donald's burden to be heard.

" Right let's get him. This way," shouted Collins running towards the dying sound. It was coming from the hillside behind the village. As they ran towards the faint sound it stopped. Clearly Donald had put the still down somewhere.

With only a vague idea of the general direction of the last sound there was no point in going out onto the heather-clad hillside in the dark.

Furiously Collins yelled, " I'll get you yet Cameron, I'll have you in jail you...you ...you thief"

Turning to yell at the other gaugers he saw a sight which quietened him instantly. There, carrying lanterns and torches was a fair crowd of the people of Foss, roused from their beds by the noise and all of them seemed to the gauger to be smiling at him. Silently, smoulderingly he led the others back into the inn. He would have that damned smuggler Cameron if it was the last thing he did, he thought grimly to himself.

Collins never got the chance. After hiding the still in the heather that night, Donald came back for it a few days later. He was pretty much a hero to the local people after the trick he had played on the gaugers. Everyone he met had heard of his exploit and he had several offers of working with other smugglers. But the whole episode had helped him to get things clear in his own mind. Oh, he had enjoyed putting one over on the gaugers as much as ever, and he was glad to accept the congratulations of his peers, but he needed a change. He was sick of being stuck in a bothy tending to the still in the smoke and heat while outside birds sang, the burns gurgled through the glens, salmon leapt and rutting stags roared on the high hills. He had other skills he could put to use.

So, to general disbelief round Lochs Tay and Rannoch, Donald Dubh Cameron sold his still and turned his skills elsewhere. The fun of outwitting gaugers was no better than the fun he could have outwitting gamekeepers and water-bailiffs. He turned all his energies to the poaching - a life that suited him well. Soon, instead of being cursed by gaugers Donald was being cursed by the protectors of the fish, birds and deer on the big Highland estates. And the water-bailiffs and the gamekeepers had no more success in trying to catch Donald than the gaugers.

Geordie White, the Glenesk Smuggler

The Reverend William Inglis sat by his study window in the manse at Tarfside in Glenesk. Outside, the hills were white with snow and the winter air was clear and crisp. The morning sun shone brightly on the scene. The river, the North Esk, had a covering of ice over much of its course through the glen. It was weather to make people stick by the fire, he thought. Sipping gently at the glass of peatreek in his hand he started thinking of the new gauger who had been appointed at the New Year. It was now the third week in January and he had been informed that the new man would be coming up Glenesk sometime soon. A devout and caring man who was very popular with his flock, William was troubled. The old gauger Colin Wyllie had been a canny man and had rarely caused much bother in the glen.

The minister knew that Wyllie had had some sort of arrangement with the smugglers, but he had never wanted to know the details. He assumed that Geordie White was involved, but it was better for a man in his position not to know too much. Geordie's peatreek was famous throughout Glenesk and its neighbouring Angus Glens and also found a ready market in Edzell, Fettercairn and Brechin, down in the plains that formed Strathmore and the Mearns. He was justifiably proud of the whisky he made, thought the minister as he took another sip. It was the real stuff, but what would this new gauger do? William had long ago stopped bothering himself about whether or not a man in his position should be a customer of such a notorious smuggler as Geordie White. He simply never talked against the smugglers from the pulpit - he was no hypocrite.

No, he enjoyed the traditional spirit of the Highland Gael and had in fact become friends with Geordie, who, apart from his dedication to distilling whisky, was as straightforward and honest a man as he had ever met. He had told Geordie to be on his guard the previous Sunday after service but Geordie had seemed unperturbed. Maybe he thought the new man would be

Tales of Whisky and Smuggling

as amenable as Wyllie had been, but Inglis had a feeling this wouldn't be the case.

Geordie was well known, too well known. Glenesk was still a regular route between Donside and the country to the south and Geordie had customers in both directions. There was little possibility that the new man would not have heard of Geordie White soon after taking over as gauger for the eastern Angus glens. Geordie was so successful he had taken to distributing other men's whisky as well as his own. The minister had no objections to any of his flock being financially successful, in fact it delighted him, but he had a feeling that something was going to go wrong.

"Ach never mind," he told himself. " No gauger is going to come up here when it is as cold as this."

Having reassured himself, the minister sat down by the blazing log fire, glass in hand and turned his mind to the next Sunday's sermon - a different kind of problem entirely.

However, the new gauger, Gordon Douglas, had no fear of the weather. Raised on a hill-top farm in the Borders he was used to the cold and had decided to use the deep snow and biting weather to his own advantage.

Just as the minister sat by the fire the gauger was making his way up past Gannachy at the foot of the glen. As he led his horse through the deep snow he was thinking of a few days before.

" The best thing you could do, Douglas," Supervisor Begg had told him in his Brechin office, " is to catch that slippery smuggler Geordie White, up there at Greenburn in Glenesk."

" Has he caused you trouble in the past?" he had asked.

" Trouble? trouble?" snorted Begg. " That man is the bane of my life Douglas.. Your predecessor Wyllie, was always just about to catch him - but he never did." He snorted again. " Huh, I'm sure there was something there.... never mind that. This Geordie White is known all over the area. He has customers all over the place, some of them gentry, and there's more than one manse that has a flask of his whisky in the cupboard. And some of the Justices of the Peace are as bad. He's been a thorn in my flesh for years. But we have him now. One of his smuggling friends has had enough of his cockiness. He has told me where the insolent swine has his still at the moment. I am sorry there's no one else around today or we could maybe even go and arrest him now. Once the snow has cleared a bit, we'll go in and get that bandit."

" I have no objection to going after smugglers in this weather, sir," he had said, sure that if the weather turned bad he could find shelter somewhere. The country people might all be on the side of the smugglers but they would never deny shelter to someone caught out in a blizzard.

96

Geordie White, the Glenesk Smuggler

The Supervisor looked long and hard at the man before him. He was tall, well built, fair-haired and with the weather-beaten features of a man used to being out in all weathers. The man was new to the area, but that could be to their advantage.

" You have no idea of the country yet," Begg had told him.

"I'm sure we can find a map that is adequate to our purpose sir," Douglas had replied.

Impressed by his new gauger's obvious commitment, Begg had agreed that the time to strike was now, when the smuggler least expected it. So it had been decided to strike quickly and now Douglas was on his way to the small farm a few miles up this snow and ice-bound glen. This smuggler was unbelievable - he had grown so cocky he had brought his still down into his house! And the house was by the river near the main glen road. It would take time to go the few more miles but then he would have the Glenesk smuggler. No one knew he was the new gauger and in this weather no-one would be able to get ahead of him without being seen, to warn the smuggler there was a stranger in the glen. In fact, it was so cold that no one was about and Douglas passed up the glen unseen.

Up at Greenburn, Geordie White and his son Alexander were tending the still set up in an outhouse of their small steading on the other side of the North Esk from Greenburn Croft. They had had a wee break after the busy New Year celebrations when Geordie's product, as always, had been in great demand. For the past ten days they had been back at the still - business as usual. There were orders to be filled. Customers were waiting. The first that Geordie knew of his danger was when he heard a shout from outside. He stuck his head outside the building's door. There on the other side of the ford across the ice-covered, fast-running river was a man on a horse. A stranger. At once he remembered what Mr. Inglis had told him. There had been a new gauger appointed. He had thought to wait awhile before taking precautions but now here he was just fifteen yards away on the other side of the river. He had to think fast. Reaching behind him and grabbing a pitchfork from behind the door, Geordie stepped out and went down to the river.

" Good afternoon, sir, can I be helping you?" he said loudly, aware of Alexander peeking out behind him.

" Yes. Tell me what is the depth of the water here," the gauger said.

With an air of innocence, but inwardly cursing whoever had informed on him, Geordie said, " Oh no, no, sir, you've come the wrong road. This is no ford, you would be drowned if you tried to cross here."

The gauger looked straight at his man. This was Geordie White all right. The balding head fringed with white hair, the prominent nose, the long arms and slightly bandy legs all fitted the description he had been given. He looked doubtful. " I was told this was the ford," replied Douglas . " Let me see the depth.

" Aye well, there's no bottom here at all , I will be showing you," called Geordie, moving right to the edge of the river. Breaking the ice with the heel of his shoe he proceeded to stick the pitchfork into the water, carefully, keeping the stick right in front of him. Angling the pitchfork carefully Geordie stuck it under the ice until half his arm was also in the water.

From the other side of the river it looked to Douglas like the staff had gone straight down. In fact the water was no more than a foot deep.

Convinced that trying to cross the ice-cold river would be suicidal, Douglas spoke again. " How near is the nearest ford or bridge then?" he demanded.

" Well now," replied Geordie," the next safe place to cross is up the glen a bit at Keenie, I would be thinking."

" And how far is that, man?" Douglas asked, gritting his teeth in frustration.

" Och it's a mile or two. Just keep going up the glen till you come to the houses at Modlach. The road to the ford is just past there. If you have any trouble finding your way, just ask," Geordie was saying when Douglas whirled his horse and headed north along the road through the lightly packed snow.

As soon as he had gone Geordie turned to Alexander," Quick Alex, douse that fire and start shifting the stuff that's ready. I'll handle the still."

By now Mrs White had come from the house and was hitching a pony to their peat cart. Within minutes the cart was loaded with peatreek and, handling the still-hot equipment with folded sacks, Geordie soon had the dismantled still on the cart too. The contents had already disappeared in the swirling river. He then drove the cart through the ford and followed the gauger's trail up the glen. He was heading for a spot he had used to hide his produce before. This was in the woods by the river only a few hundred yards away. By the time Douglas had got to the ford at Keenie and come back down the west side of the river he had covered well over five miles. The White family had covered over the cart tracks on the other side of the river and when the gauger arrived there was nothing incriminating to be found.

After a fruitless search of the steading, Douglas was about to ride back up to Keenie when Geordie asked innocently, " Och, why don't you just cross back over here. It'll save you a bit of time."

Douglas was absolutely speechless.

Geordie of course moved his still away from the house up into the hills after this, realising how close a shave he had had. From then on he was extra careful.

Geordie White, the Glenesk Smuggler

Although it was unforgivable for a Minister of the Church to advocate law-breaking the Reverend Inglis found the story hilarious. After the service the next Sunday he had a word with Geordie.

" Well, Geordie," he said. " I believe you had a visitor during the week."

" Och it was nobody to speak of Minister," the elderly smuggler innocently replied. "It was just some gauger loon that didn't know his way around. I soon put him on the right track though."

Supervisor Begg was furious when he heard the news. His plan of sending the unknown gauger had backfired and now he realised that Douglas should have had a local to guide him. His determination to arrest White grew even stronger. Douglas' newness to the area was no longer of any advantage.

When spring came, he brought in a gauger from near Perth. This was a man called Holder who had been successful around Glenalmond.

Carefully getting in touch with his informer in Glenesk, Begg soon had a rough idea of where Geordie's new still was located. Geordie hadn't managed to find out who had told on him and the man had been pleased to help the gaugers again - for a price. It was somewhere near the top of the Holmhead burn on the slopes of the Bulg, the hill behind Geordie's steading.

Holder was sent to approach the area through the next glen to the west, Glen Lethnot, approaching over the Hill of Wirran. It was about noon when he came past Craiganower to the shoulder of the Bulg. There ahead of him he could see a thin column of smoke. This seemed all too easy.

Carefully picking his way through the knee-high heather Holder moved round the hill towards the smoke. After twenty minutes he was within a hundred yards of the bothy. He could see the smoke, which seemed to be coming from a hole in the ground alongside the Holmhead burn. Slowly and carefully he moved forward. Soon, he was almost at the bothy, but there was still no sign other than the smoke. He crept even closer. At last he could make out the shape of the bothy. It was cunningly built into a natural hollow alongside the burn. He had him now.

Confidently, Holder ripped open the camouflaged door of the bothy and stepped in, saying, " You are under arrest George White for contravention of the Excise laws."

As calm as always, the elderly, balding Geordie looked at the gauger and asked, " Did anyone see you come in here?"

Full of himself at having managed to catch the notorious Geordie White red-handed Holder replied, " No , no one saw me."

Smiling, Geordie picked up an axe from the bothy floor and, holding it in both hands said, " Ach well no one will see you going out either then."

" My God," thought the gauger, " he's going to murder me." At once, he turned on his heels and fled from the bothy. Behind him, Geordie was laughing at how easily he had fooled the poor man - he would never have used the axe, but the gauger didn't know that. He didn't stop till he was over a mile away, heading back the way he had come. When at last he stopped to catch his breath he was convinced that he had had a narrow escape. His sense of relief was tempered by concern over what Begg would say. Faced by a single smuggler, he had turned and run - he would be lucky to keep his position. There was only one option. He would have to say he couldn't find the bothy. That was it, he would say there was no bothy by the Holmhead burn. Begg would just have to take his word for it.

There was an added bonus for Geordie in all this. Begg was so furious when he was told he had been misinformed that he immediately rode to Glenesk and went to the home of the informer, a near neighbour of Geordie's called Henderson who lived at Dalhastnie. Henderson had never managed to make peatreek of any quality and Geordie had refused to distribute it on several occasions. This was the source of the man's hatred and subsequent informing.

The news of the Supervisor's arrival in the glen spread like wildfire and unknown to Begg when he demanded the return of the money paid from Henderson, there were several pairs of ears noting every word. Henderson could only repay part of the money and despite his protestations that the still was where he had said, Begg told him he was lucky not to be jailed for giving false information. After the Supervisor had gone back down the glen, Henderson received a visit from a group of his neighbours. He wasn't harmed but the following day was seen leaving Glenesk forever.

Later that same year, Geordie was down in Brechin. He had come in with a cartload of hay and nothing else. The peatreek he was supplying to his thirsty Brechin customers was in another cart which was being driven by a neighbour. Once in the town the two men met up in a courtyard off the High Street to distribute their wares. They had already checked with Geordie's contacts that there were no gaugers around. Carrying an anker of whisky Geordie was heading down the hill when he saw a familiar figure coming out of a house and up the hill towards him. It was none other than gauger Douglas. This was a tricky situation. As the gauger came closer Geordie stopped and rested his anker of whisky on a low wall.

"Good day Mr.Douglas," he said with a smile. " It's a warm day for this time of the year. In fact I would be glad if you would relieve me of this whisky, it's terrible heavy and I'm fair tired carrying it."

Douglas glowered at Geordie, " Damn you White, have you nothing better to do than try to humiliate me. You would love it if I arrested you now

- you have none of your damned spirits in that barrel. You will not make me a laughing stock again. Get out of my way," he growled, shoving Geordie out of the way and heading up the hill.

" As you wish Mr Douglas, sir," Geordie called after him, shaking with relief that he had got away with yet another trick. That one had been too close for comfort. He was glad indeed to deliver the rest of the whisky and get back to Glenesk that day.

A Nasty Piece of Work

Not all of those involved in making and distributing the peatreek were decent human beings. Though many of the people involved, men and women, were quite prepared to defend their product with violence if the gaugers came upon them, very few were out-and-out criminals. Most of them truly thought that the government had no right to try and deprive them of their ancient whisky-making traditions. Although the late eighteenth and early nineteenth centuries were a period of great economic and social change, the majority of people in Scotland still lived in villages and hamlets. Most folk, especially in the Highlands, still existed in a subsistence economy. Money had not yet become universal and the small communities were in many respects self-sufficient. They grew most of their own food and (with a healthy if somewhat monotonous diet by today's standards) relied upon travelling tailors, shoemakers and so on for those things they could not make themselves. So it was natural for them to make their own drink, whether ale or whisky. And as the need for money spread, mainly by money rent being demanded instead of payment in kind, the peatreek was the easiest answer. Therefore the greatest number of the folk involved in the manufacture and distribution, of the peatreek were normal, law-abiding people in all other respects.

However, there were exceptions. There were those who cared little for the quality of the whisky they made and were concerned only with profit. Among these were those who were as ruthless as they were unscrupulous.

One of these was a man called Thomas McDonald who came initially from Glen Banchor near Newtonmore in the Badenoch district. Even as a lad he had been wild and by the time he was a regular member of south bound peatreek convoys towards the end of the Napoleonic wars he already had a reputation as a short-tempered and vicious individual. He was tall, broad, red-haired, with a fixed glower on his face. Like all of the men who went with the convoys he carried a bludgeon or club. This was acceptable, especially as they were up against sword-carrying gaugers who often had pistols too. McDonald's club though, was unusual. He had carefully studded it with nails, making it a fearsome weapon indeed. His companions thought this was nasty but no-one said much.

The standard behaviour of the convoy members after a successful "run" was to hold a wild party on returning home. These parties could last for days, a vast supply of whisky being available, and fights often broke out among the drunken "flaskers". Most of these fights were short and all would be forgiven when the antagonists sobered up - a not unusual state of affairs even nowadays. McDonald, though, never forgave a slight and after one particularly wild party had fallen out with a giant of a man called Ewan Rennie. Having got the worse of it, McDonald harboured a deep resentment. Wanting revenge, he waited a few days after the party and waylaid Rennie one night on his way back home near Newtonmore.

He leapt from cover, felled the big Highlandman from behind and was about to club him again, when he was surprised by two of Rennie's neighbours coming up the road behind him. Forced to run off, McDonald soon realised that the whole country was against him.

Rennie was well liked and McDonald's treacherous assault had made all men his enemy. Managing to collect a little money and a few belongings from his family in Glen Banchor he thought it wise to leave the district. He headed south to the Trossachs where he knew a few smugglers. He had met them on previous expeditions and though they thought him a bit coarse none of them was aware at first of just how nasty he could be.

The camaraderie of the peatreek ensured him a place and within a few months he was busy running his own still. It was situated in a wood on Beinn Dearg to the north of Port of Menteith. He was no great distiller but such was the demand for spirits in the great city of Glasgow to the south that he managed to sell all he could make. He took little care over his peatreek but as he was prepared to drink the stuff himself none of the other smugglers felt it right to say anything. He had regular contact with a group of ruffians in the city who ran a *shebeen* or illicit drinking den, and were happy to get any liquor they could. They gave him the name Tom Badenoch.

About this time there was a roving gauger or Ranger called David Dougal operating in the area. Hard but fair, Dougal was respected by the smugglers. A small, wiry man with greying hair and a neatly trimmed beard, his most obvious characteristic was his piercing grey eyes. He was successful in confiscating spirits and his sharp wit and sense of fair play had made him very few enemies amongst the smuggling fraternity. To Tom Badenoch, however, all gaugers were the same - they were his enemies and as such despicable.

One night, Dougal was walking along the the road from Fintry to Arnprior in the shadow of the Gargunnock Hills. He knew of Tom Badenoch and had received information that he was on his way along this particular road. Dougal was a brave man but not a foolish one so he decided to be careful. There was no advantage to be gained by being careless when dealing with a villain like McDonald. He was walking north just off the road, leading his horse, when he saw a figure crouched behind the roadside wall up ahead. Leaving his horse he crept a bit closer. The figure turned out to be Tom Badenoch himself, priming a pistol. This was unusual indeed. Very rarely did any of the smugglers resort to arms. They knew this would bring down even greater force against them from the government - a government still not rid of the fears engendered by the French Revolution. Smuggling was one thing, but the idea of an armed uprising was never far from the thoughts of the government's members in London. If the smugglers resorted to firearms things would change fast, and they knew it.

Tom Badenoch, though, cared for no one but himself. Growing greedier and more determined to sell his peatreek he had prevailed upon his so-called friends in Glasgow to get him a pistol. No damned gauger would get his whisky! He had heard in the local inn that a Ranger was hanging about the area and had decided to be ready for him.

Watching from behind a tree, Dougal could see no sign of any whisky. It must be hidden up the road a bit. Dougal himself was unarmed apart from a stout staff. Suddenly he had a thought. Pulling his spyglass from his coat pocket, he held it before him like a pistol and stepped out from behind a tree. Running at Badedoch he called, " Right then smuggler I'm ready for you. Surrender in the King's name."

Badenoch looked up to see the gauger running at him, pistol in hand. Vicious and grasping though he was, he was no coward. There was no way he would surrender. He fired at Dougal and missed. With a roar of frustration he leapt over the wall he was hiding behind and took off up the road. Close behind him came Dougal. He had no intention of giving the man time to reload. Suddenly, there was Badenoch's pony with four ankers on its back. The smuggler ran right past it, expecting to be shot at any moment. Dougal reached the pony, which was ready to bolt and, calming it down, headed back to his own horse. He had no doubt that Badenoch would soon realise he wan't being chased and come back - with his pistol loaded. So, mounting up he headed off with the whisky-laden pony. Badenoch did come back down the road a few minutes later, by which time Dougal was well on his way.

It wasn't long before the story spread of how the great Tom Badenoch had been fooled by a gauger with his spyglass. Many of the smugglers had a higher respect for Dougal than for McDonald anyway and the big Badenoch man was soon the subject of a deal of coarse humour. Furious at how he had been tricked, he let it be known that he would have his revenge. The few friends he had all told him to forget all about it and get back to business, but he was adamant.

Several of the smugglers warned the gauger that his life was in danger. They would never turn informer, but realised that killing a gauger would make things hot for them all. And of course more than a few of them had an intense dislike for ther ruthless and vicious Tom Badenoch.

Gauger Dougal was not one to be troubled by threats. Having got the best of the smuggler once, he was sure he could do so again if necessary but just to be on the safe side, he too began carrying a pistol.

Badenoch was no fool and decided to do nothing for a while. If he let things return to normal for a while maybe he could catch Dougal off his guard. So for a while he went back to making and selling his whisky and even stopped muttering threats against Dougal. Every so often, remarks would be passed about spyglasses in his company but McDonald managed to control his temper. A couple of months passed and some of the smugglers even began to think that the wild man from Badenoch was going to let matters rest. It was even suggested that he might be mellowing with age and experience, but few thought this a real possibility. With the passing weeks the spyglass affair and how Badenoch would have his revenge became less and less of a talking point. There was always some new trick played upon the gaugers to keep tongues wagging. Gauger Dougal continued to have a remarkable level of success in locating stills and catching smugglers. As ever he would go off on his own for days at a time and his fellow gaugers were used to this.

One day however the inevitable happened. A young cowherd called Willie Campbell was driving a handful of cows up by the Keltie Water near Callander when he saw what he thought was a bundle of clothes on the path ahead. Telling his dog, Dubh, to watch the cattle he strode ahead. As he came close he began to realise that this pathetic heap was in fact a body, battered almost beyond recognition. As he realised this Willie felt sick and fell to his knees retching. There was obviously nothing to be done for the poor soul so, after a few deep breaths, Willie ran into the nearby town of Callander to tell of what he had seen.

Soon the resident gauger, John Malcolm, the local Justice of the Peace and a crowd of interested locals came with a horse and cart to collect the grisly remains.

Tales of Whisky and Smuggling

Bending over the bloodstained and twisted corpse, Malcolm swallowed hard and said, " It's Dougal the Ranger, someone has battered him to death. He's in a hell of a mess." At that, he got up, walked away a bit and he too was sick.

Despite a thorough search roundabout there was no evidence of a fight. The only conclusion was that he had been murdered elsewhere and brought to this spot and dumped. There was not a scrap of evidence as to who the guilty person was. The Supervisor came up from Crieff with half-a-dozen other gaugers but they too found nothing. It was two weeks later that something did turn up. Dougal's spyglass, wallet and clasp-knife were found by a small lochan high up on Ben Vorlich miles to the north. Here too there were no signs of a struggle, but the heavy rains of the previous days had probably washed them away. The gaugers had no evidence at all as to who the murderer was, so there was no one they could arrest.

The smugglers knew who had killed Dougal. They needed no evidence to be sure that Tom McDonald from Badenoch had surprised Dougal on the slopes of Ben Vorlich and battered him to death with his nail-studded bludgeon.

A few days after Dougal's body was found, Tom Badenoch went to call on a bothy not far from his own. As he entered, one of the two men tending the still looked up at him and said, " You are not welcome here Badenoch and never will be again, get out."

His companion had picked up an axe and was looking coldly at the big Highlander. Sneering, McDonald did as he was told. Everywhere he went the same thing happened. No one was prepared even to talk to him. Though gaugers were sometimes killed, and smugglers too, in the heat of battle over barrels of peatreek, this was different. Dougal had been a fair and honest man and this vicious, unprincipled villain had murdered him. It was cold-blooded and premeditated. From that time on Tom Badenoch was an outcast. No-one would talk to him and no-one would sell him the materials he needed to run his still. Even his contacts in Glasgow realised that the countryside was against him. They dealt with too many others to risk anything for one such as him.

Known for centuries for their hospitality, the Highland Scots were an honourable and proud people. This crime was unforgivable and every man and woman's hand was turned against the murdering smuggler. For a few weeks he could be seen wandering alone in the foothills of the Perthshire mountains but then he was seen no more.

The following spring a badly decomposed body was found huddled among some rocks on the slopes of Ben Vorlich. By the side of the body was a nail-studded bludgeon. Wandering, despised by all, Tom Badenoch had died alone on the hillside not far from the spot where it seemed he had brutally murdered the Ranger. Only then did the Supervisor of Revenue at Crieff find out who had killed David Dougal. There might not have been enough evidence to convict and hang the murderer, but the smugglers needed no evidence or court of law. They were an integral part of the community they supplied and the whole community had meted out the justice they all agreed was deserved.

Village by the Sidlaws

The village of Auchterhouse sits at the foot of the Sidlaw hills five miles north west of Dundee. In the peatreek's greatest years, Auchterhouse was a hotbed of smuggling activity. There were smugglers a-plenty in and around the village and convoys of Highland smugglers regularly arrived on the way to sell their wares in Dundee or in Fife. The road to Blairgowrie and beyond to Dunkeld and Braemar ran past the village and in the hills to the north-east of the village was Glen Ogilvy, a favourite track of the Highland smugglers. On moonlit nights, long convoys of whisky-laden Highland shelties would come down through Glen Ogilvy, just as a hundred years before the same places had seen Highland caterans or cattle-raiders heading north with lifted cattle. Although by the turn of the nineteenth century the people of Auchterhouse no longer spoke the Gaelic they still had strong ties with their Highland cousins, ties that were maintained by their common involvement with the peatreek.

Convoys of peatreek from as far away as Lochaber regularly arrived in and around Auchterhouse to empty the contents of the twenty-pint barrels into smaller containers - flagons, bladder-skins and bottles - which would then be taken into the nearby city for sale. Other convoys would head down to Invergowrie and ferry their wares over to Fife.

As one inhabitant said, thirty years after the heyday of the peatreek, "They were awfie drouthie (awfully thirsty) the Fife folk then, whatever they may be now. They would tak as much drink in Fife as they could run across!" The elderly ex-smuggler then added with a wink, " We were aa (all) in it then."

Right enough, in the early nineteenth century it seems virtually the entire population of Auchterhouse, which was several hundred people, was involved. The ministers sons, George and Duncan Scott, often helped the convoys shift their product while they were in their teens. Known as a pair of wild young lads they were often summoned from their beds by a tap on their bedroom window. They would spring up, keen to help the smugglers in their night-time work. In later life these two could hardly have been more respectable, George becoming an admiral and Duncan a general. The wages for such work were invariably paid in peatreek, wages which were gladly accepted by all involved. Although the long, dark nights of winter were the busiest time for tending the sma' stills, there being less labour needed on the land, the business continued all year round.

The Sidlaws were full of carefully hidden bothies and it was a common pastime for young men to come from Dundee and the nearby villages on Sunday afternoons for a picnic in the hills. The gaugers were of course off duty on Sundays and the bothies did a brisk trade. The smugglers would wander round selling whisky from flagons to all who wanted it and there were many who had trouble getting the few miles home after a Sunday afternoon in the Sidlaws! One giant Highland smuggler wandered around wearing a flagon of whisky shaped like a dragoon's *cuirass* or breastplate. This receptacle had a small tap at the bottom to dispense the amber nectar within. Once the transaction was complete, the smuggler would simply close the big overcoat he wore summer and winter, and pass on to his next customer.

Of course the gaugers knew that Auchterhouse was a hotbed of smuggling and regularly raided the village and the hills behind. However like everywhere else in Scotland at the time, they had a difficult job as everybody rallied round to stop the preventive officers achieving success. Sometimes, however they were successful in locating bothies and convoys and the result was often a pitched battle between the gaugers and the smugglers.

One of the finest makers of peatreek was a lady of some years called Mrs. Watson. She came of a long line of smugglers, her grandfather and her father having been very active in the trade. She came initially from Athole, where her mother's family were especially well known for their skill with the sma' still. Even as a child she was involved.

" Och I could only have been seven or eight and was ill in bed with a fever,' she was telling a neighbour one time, " and father had four small ankers of fresh stuff in the house, as well as a bag of malt ready to take to the still, when the gaugers arrived. They had come over the hills and surprised us. There was no time at all to lose but father had the right idea. Quick as you like, he lifted me and the mattress from the box-bed, put the *poit dubh* and the malt in the bed and replaced the mattress. I was put back on top, told what to say and when the door burst open a minute later the gaugers saw my mother and father leaning over me in my bed. As they came in to search the house I began to moan. Over came the preventive man and says to father, " What's wrong with her?" and father replied , "Och but she has an awful fever. We're at our wit's end. Here feel her brow yourself," and he took the gauger's hand as if to put it on my head. Och you would have thought the poor creature had been stung. He pulled his hand back and he and his fellows were out of there like a shot. I played my part well that day and many a good laugh we had at that afterwards."

Mrs. Watson, who had been widowed in her thirties, was still active in her sixties and her finest helper was her horse. This was Punch, a fine white beast that was as eager as his mistress to get off to the bothy. This might just have been because Punch enjoyed eating the *draff* or leftovers from the still and drinking the lees or *brunt drink*. However Mrs. Watson said she made sure he never drank too much. Punch was invaluable in taking her to the bothy, carrying back her whisky and being an extra pair of ears and eyes. There was little chance of the gaugers sneaking up on her bothy with Punch there. Mrs. Watson maintained that she could leave Punch at the door watching the *browst* while she had a wee sleep. If anything untoward happened the horse would neigh loudly and waken her.

" Ach Punch is the best helper I've ever had in the bothy," she would say with a smile.

The smugglers were of course busiest on Saturdays and Sundays, most of them having other work to do during the week, on the land or about the home. One of Mrs. Watson's neighbours on the hill was Davie McDonald, also from Auchterhouse. His bothy was well above hers on the same burn and she always knew when he was working by the run off in the stream. One October Sunday, however she got an awful shock. It was a wild day with squalls of rain and a wind coming from the east. Busy at her own *browst* with the faithful Punch at the door, she went outside to escape the smoke for a minute and looked casually at the stream. It was an unnatural colour. It wasn't the dark brown caused by the run off from McDonald's still but a pale golden colour. She knew that colour all too well. The burn was running with whisky.

Up the hill, Davie Stewart and his two sons had just filled a barrel of whisky from their still when the gaugers came upon them. They had come close unseen because of the blowy, squally weather. They were led by the notorious James MacNicol, a Highlander from the far north who had for some reason joined the gaugers. He was considered a traitor by all the smugglers, especially as he was highly successful at his job.

The first the Stewarts knew of the gaugers was when the door burst open and MacNicol stood in the doorway with three other gaugers behind him.

" Hand over that whisky in the name of the King," roared MacNicol, a hefty man in his late twenties.

110

"At them lads," called Davie, with no hesitation.

The three Stewarts rushed at MacNicol, bowling him over and into the men behind. At once a desperate fight broke out. The Stewarts had no intention of giving up the peatreek. The gaugers had short staffs and the Stewarts had grabbed whatever was to hand as they rushed out of the bothy. Sticks and paddles flew. Thuds and cries rang out. Briefly the battle raged but all too soon the gaugers had the upper hand. Within minutes, Davie and his son Iain were stretched out unconscious and Jamie, the younger son had his arms pinned behind his back by one of the gaugers. Quickly his hands were bound.

" Right," said MacNicol, grinning despite the blood flowing from a wound on his scalp," go back for the horses Wilson and we'll have this lot of whisky away with us. A good day's work lads."

" That's as maybe, but look over there," replied Wilson, pointing off to the left.

The noise of the battle had been heard at a bothy further up the hillside on another burn and word had spread like wildfire that gaugers were attacking the Stewarts. Coming down towards them were nearly a dozen smugglers, all clutching sticks and clubs. They were still a few hundred yards off. Time was of the essence. There was no way to get the whisky away. Ducking into the bothy MacNicol reappeared almost instantly carrying a barrel.

" We'll not let these devils get the whisky. Smash the barrels lads," he called, lifting the barrel and throwing it at a large boulder in the burn. The barrel smashed into pieces, the contents flowing away down the burn. One of the gaugers found an axe and the others used MacNicol's technique. In a couple of minutes all of the barrels were smashed, their contents running away down the hillside in the burn. Young Jamie could only look on and groan.

With the roars of the other smugglers growing louder as they approached McNicol said to his men, " Away back to the horses lads, I''ll slow them up." Whipping a pistol from his belt he fired a shot towards the approaching group. They threw themselves flat in the heather and the gauger turned and ran after his comrades. The smugglers were still over a hundred yards away through the heather and with this head start MacNicol and his men got safely away.

A few months after this, MacNicol heard of a large convoy coming down from Lochaber. This time the convoy was heading towards the village of Bridgefoot, a couple of miles north of Dundee, where they intended transferring their whisky into smaller receptacles. With the hard, cold, snowy weather and the celebrations of Hogmanay not too far off there was a

111

lot of business waiting to be done. In all, the convoy was carrying several hundred gallons of whisky and there were about forty ponies and upwards of twenty smugglers in the convoy. MacNicol was waiting on the nearby farm of Old Baldragon. With him he had a dozen gaugers and a company of dragoons. He intended waiting until the whisky was being transferred and then he would swoop. That way he would get the whisky, the members of the convoy and the local people who were helping them. He had taken great care that no one had left the farm after he and his wee army had got there. What he didn't know was that they had been spotted by the local publican at Downfield as they passed on their way from Dundee. He was waiting for supplies from the convoy and sent his son across country to warn them.

The convoy was headed by a giant, red-haired man known far and wide as the "Bairn" or baby. He had been given the name because, gigantic as he was, over six and a half feet tall and built to match, he was the smallest of six brothers called MacMaster, from Glen Loy in far Lochaber. Although feared by the gaugers because of his size and reputation as a wild man he was in fact a gentle soul and slow to anger. He was walking along the road towards Bridgefoot just past the ancient Pictish symbol stone known as Martin's Stone when the young lad came running up. The convoy was a couple of hundred yards behind. Snow was beginning to fall as the Bairn heard the news of the trap. Thanking the young lad, he turned and ran back to the convoy. Normally if there had just been gaugers ahead, armed or not, he would have pressed on but the dragoons being with MacNicol altered the odds too much.

Calling to the lead man of the convoy in Gaelic he said, " There is a party of gaugers and dragoons ahead, let us be going over to Auchterhouse. I am sure our friends there will help us hide the stuff."

At once the column veered off to the west through the fields. Soon they were on the road into Auchterhouse with a man sent ahead to tell the villagers what was happening. There was no doubt that the gaugers would soon realise that the convoy had turned aside and would scour the whole area. The bairn headed straight for the house of Jeannie Gray, an old friend with whom he had done much business himself. Jeannie, a buxom, handsome, dark-haired woman in her early fifties knew just what to do. The smugglers were split up into groups and each group was sent to a different house. Jeannie was no mean smuggler herself and knew a few tricks. Her still was in fact underneath her kitchen. Unfortunately for the Bairn, that was full of her own peatreek at the moment.

" Ach well Bairn, we'll just have to try something else. Could you get your lads to shift the woodpile at the side of the house?" she asked.

" Och certainly we can do that, but will they not look there, the government men?' he replied in his lilting English.

" Maybe, maybe not," Jean smiled and winked.

Within a matter of a few minutes the wood pile was moved, the whisky put against the side of the house and the wood restacked over it. The snow was falling heavier by the minute and ten minutes after the job was done the woodpile was well-covered with a fine white blanket, getting thicker by the minute. A few other barrels were hidden in underground cellars, hayricks and even a few in a dungheap. All were soon hidden by the snow.

Laughing happily, the big Highlander gave Jean a hug, then he and his men headed out of the village with the ponies to hide out up in the hills. By the time MacNicol had figured out where the Highlanders might have gone they were well into the hills. Coming into Auchterhouse with his troop he could see no sign of the convoy. He well knew the extent of local support for the convoys and ordered a search. Not a Highlandman, a spare pony nor any of the whisky was to be seen. It was getting very cold indeed and though the Highlanders up in the hills were used to the weather and could stay there for days, the gaugers and dragoons had no intention of heading up into the Sidlaws in what could easily turn into a blizzard. In fact, most of the Highlanders had gone to a couple of the bothies and were sitting by blazing fires while the dragoons and gaugers shivered in the snow.

MacNicol was forced to admit defeat since the dragoons were becoming restive. If they had come to the village on their own they knew they would have been given a dram or two of peatreek to keep out the cold but there was no chance of that with the gaugers about.

Over the next few days, the weather didn't ease up but as ever there were sturdy farmwives seen heading into town with pails of milk yoked over their shoulders. Quite a few of them were pails with false bottoms containing bladders of peatreek. Carts of peat and firewood continued to supply the city folk. Many of the carts too contained bottles and bladderskins of the Bairn's peatreek, along with the Auchterhouse product. And hardly a woman went to town without a couple of the bladder skins under her dress. MacNicol and his gaugers were riding all of the roads around the Sidlaws looking for the convoy which had faded away back to Lochaber in ones or twos, leaving the Bairn and a couple of others to see to collecting their money.

The following spring, gauger MacNicol had a bit more success. He was out with two colleagues early one March morning looking around on the slopes of Balkello Hill north-east of Auchterhouse. Walking up the banks of the Linn of Balluderon they came across nine and a half ankers of peatreek, hidden under the overhanging bank of the burn. Staying with the find MacNicol sent one of the others down to North Balluderon farm to obtain a horse and cart. The man was soon back, the whisky loaded and the three gaugers set off back towards Dundee. Just past the spot where the Bairn had heard of the gauger's ambush those few months before they had to pass Wyntoun wood. As they drove past, three powerful Highlanders ran out of the wood throwing stones and waving sticks. Down jumped the gaugers and fierce hand-to-hand fighting began. All of them were armed with sticks and the cut and thrust was hard and fast. Soon all of them were bleeding. Suddenly one of the gaugers fell.

MacNicol was having difficulty keeping his man at bay and saw his other companion fall under the combined blows of the two smugglers. He thought he was next and redoubled his efforts forcing his assailant back a bit. The other two smugglers grabbed two ankers apiece from the cart and hurried off. Still the last one came at him. Then from the corner of his eye he saw one of his companions begin to rise. His concentration distracted, his opponent saw his chance. Thump! A stunning blow caught MacNicol on the left temple and he fell to his knees. As the other gauger grabbed for the weapon he had let fall the smuggler swung at him, missed but caused the gauger to slip. At once the last Highlander ran to the cart. Blood streaming from his wound, MacNicol threw himself at the man, knocking him to the ground. With the other gauger now coming at him to the smuggler rolled away from MacNicol, leapt to his feet and ran off after his friends now almost out of sight.

It was only as they helped the third gauger to his feet that the other two looked around. In the field to the east were a group of men leaning on their hoes while on the road behind a pair of carts were stopped. Their drivers too had had a clear view of the battle. Not one of them had a made a move to help the gaugers. Biting back curses, MacNicol went over to the cart. There were still six ankers there, not a bad day's haul.

Painfully, he and his friends climbed up on the cart and rode back towards Dundee. The whole episode had lasted no more than ten minutes and not a word had been spoken.

All too often, whisky that was seized was won back by the smugglers and the gaugers could never hope for help from the locals who all gave their support to the smugglers. Sometimes it wasn't only whisky that got away. Just south of Wyntoun, an Auchterhouse smuggler called Paterson had built a bothy in a thicket in the wood behind Gallowhill. He was busy at his still late one Saturday afternoon when he heard a twig snap in the wood outside. At once he sprang to the bothy door. Too late. There in front of him stood

MacNicol and another gauger, Corbett, a man well known for his enjoyment of life. Behind them were the figures of a couple of mounted dragoons. Corbett said, " Well, well Paterson we have you now. I think you should put the handcuffs on him, Mr. MacNicol and we can send him into town. You'll be spending tonight in jail Paterson," he went on.

" It's a cold day Mr. MacNicol, sir," the smuggler said as the gauger brought out handcuffs from his greatcoat pocket. " Would it be all right if I put on my coat? I'm sure you wouldn't want me catching my death of cold."

" All right, but be quick," snapped MacNicol signalling one of the dragoons to come forward. " Put these on him and take him into town," he ordered, giving the mounted trooper the handcuffs. The gauger then followed Corbett into the bothy to see what they had got. The trooper dismounted and Paterson, now with his bulky greatcoat on, shoved his hands at the dragoon. Quickly the soldier snapped the big clumsy manacles round his wrists. Too quickly. The wily Paterson had his overcoat sleeves down over his wrists as the handcuffs were shut. Corbett and MacNicol came out of the bothy.

" Right," said Corbett," he has no spirits here. The *browst* is still running. We'll let it run and come back later for the spirits. We're heading up to the hills now. You know what to do with him." So saying, the gaugers mounted the horses the other dragoon had been holding and the three of them picked their way through the wood heading north. The other dragoon sent Paterson ahead of him towards the road running down to Bridgefoot.

Walking towards Dundee Paterson kept looking about. They began to pass a copse of trees on the right. Suddenly, in a field over to the left Paterson saw a dog chasing then catching a hare.

" Hey look - over there in the field. That's a fine big hare that dog's got. It would make a fine stew that," he said over his shoulder to the trooper and pointing with his manacled hands.

" You're right. Stay there," replied the dragoon and, jumping his horse over the dyke and ditch alongside the road, he headed into the field. As soon as he turned Paterson pulled up his coat sleeves and slipped the manacles off his wrists. Dropping the handcuffs in the middle of the road he sprang into the wood and disappeared. In the field the dragoon had dismounted and taken the hare from the dog when he looked back to the road. Paterson had gone.

Cursing, the trooper remounted and galloped back. Up and down through the small wood he thrashed, swinging his sabre through the underbrush. The wily smuggler had slipped behind him over the road and was heading back to his still behind the dyke on the other side of the road. By the time the dragoon gave up in disgust and headed back towards his

Tales of Whisky and Smuggling

barracks at Dudhope in Dundee, Paterson was back at his bothy. He calmly finished his *browst*, put the whisky into a couple of ankers and by the time MacNicol and Corbett returned both he and the whisky were long gone.

Corbett, though a conscientious and dedicated man, was known to like a drink himself. When he was 'merry' he just loved to sing and his favourite song was the ballad "Sherrifmuir". Like many of the grand old Scottish ballads, it took a long while to sing its many verses and Corbett took great pleasure in making a real performance of it.

One day in 1823, Corbett was with Supervisor Henderson from Coupar Angus a few miles north west of Auchterhouse. An informer had told Corbett of a convoy coming down from the north which was set to come through the village of Meigle, nowadays on the A94 and the site of the world-famous Meigle Museum of Pictish symbol stones. They were waiting with a couple of other gaugers south of the village. Henderson was in a very good mood. A few days before with the help of a detachment of Scots Greys who were billeted at the Strathmore Inn in Coupar Angus he had siezed fifty ankers of peatreek at Kirkmichael about twenty miles to the north in Strathardle. Each anker was valued at six pounds and the two dozen ponies would be ransomed back at one pound a head. It had been a very successful raid and no one had been hurt, the presence of the Dragoons for once scaring the Highlanders off.

When the convoy hadn't materialised as dusk began to fall, Henderson suggested a short sojourn to the inn at Meigle for something to eat and perhaps a glass or two to keep out the cold.

When they arrived at the inn, one thing led to another and more than a glass or two was taken. So of course Corbett was encouraged to perform. Years of singing his favourite song had given him a real sense of the dramatic, and he was delighted to comply with the request. His voice was tuneful but, above all, it was loud.

The gaugers weren't the only ones waiting for the convoy. John Stewart of Edderty, a steading just over the hills from Auchterhouse, was a regular smuggler. He had received word a few days before that the Bairn was on his way down through Meigle and would call on him to shift some of the whisky into bladders. John had been expecting them earlier that day and as the day grew dark he had come up the road to Meigle with his horse and cart to see what was happening. As he neared the Meigle Inn he heard singing. Getting closer he recognised the song, and coming even closer he recognised the voice. Quietly, he drew to a halt near the inn got down off the cart and crept up to the inn. Looking through the window, he saw Corbett just getting into his stride and belting out the ballad, to encouragement from Henderson and the other gaugers.

Quickly he remounted his cart and was just getting out of the village when he saw the gigantic figure of the Bairn approaching.

As they met on the road John quickly told his Highland friend of the gaugers' presence.

" How close is the convoy?" he then asked.

" They are just coming behind me now," said the big smuggler as indeed the first ponies came into view.

" Quick then. If we're quiet and sharp we'll get by while Corbett's still singing," Stewart suggested.

So, as quickly and quietly as they could, the smugglers trotted their shelties past the inn and on towards Edderty. They were a good bit past the inn when the shouting and clapping told them Corbett's party piece was finished. Long before the gaugers decided to leave the inn and look for the supposed convoy, the smugglers were well out of sight. Though they didn't find the convoy that night, the gaugers still went home feeling good.

It was only a matter of time before someone let it slip to the gaugers what had happened that night at Meigle. From then on, though he still would sing 'Sherrifmuir", Corbett never quite managed to rekindle his old enthusiasm for the ballad.

In Strathmore

The valley of Strathmore runs from Perth north east for over forty miles to meet the east coast plain of The Mearns. The hills on either side, the Grampian Mountains to the north and the Sidlaws to the south, are dotted with Iron Age forts, stone circles and other monuments of the past, including Dunsinane where Macbeth, (in reality a strong and rightful king) had one of his royal residences. Strathmore itself has castles and keeps, Roman signal stations, battle sites and the mysterious symbol stones of the ancient Picts. The lush valley with the often snow clad mountains to the north has had an honourable and important role in Scottish History through the centuries. Lying between the Highlands and the valleys of the Tay and Earn, Strathmore was also a natural route for the smugglers bringing their wares down from their Highland homes for their thirsty customers to the South. An area that fits the description *hauf-hielant* (half-Highland), Strathmore had more than its fair share of native smugglers in the Peatreek years.

The local Supervisor of Excise at Coupar Angus for a good few years was a man called Joseph Henderson. With the glens of Strathardle, Glenshee and Glenisla all being in regular use by the smugglers, he had a lot of ground to cover. Apart from the smugglers distilling their peatreek in the glens themselves, there were also regular convoys from as far away as Lochaber, Badenoch and the Braes o' Mar caming down the glens. The eastern Strathmore glens - Glen Prosen, Glen Clova and Glen Esk -were also often used. To help him, Henderson had three gaugers at Coupar Angus, another three at Blairgowrie, the same at Alyth and a further three at Kirkmichael, ten miles up into the Grampians in Strathardle. In addition he had a varying number of Rangers, the roving gaugers, and from 1823-6 could call upon the Scots Greys who were billeted locally.

This detachment consisted of a sergeant and twelve troopers. Their presence was a mixed blessing for the gaugers. They were known as great consumers of the peatreek themselves and were generally reluctant to harass the smugglers, many of whom were in fact their friends.

Henderson, like all Supervisors, always went about his duties on horseback, wearing a red coat and usually with a brace of pistols in holsters on his saddle. The gaugers were sometimes mounted, sometimes on foot and had no regular uniform. Unless real trouble, was feared they were usually only armed with sticks, staves or bludgeons, which were the weapons the smugglers themselves used. The gaugers were of course selected from men of good character and some education. One of their more mundane jobs was to keep a constant check on all the public houses in their area. They would make fortnightly visits to take note of the publicans' stores and make their returns to the Commissioners of Excise in Edinburgh. The publicans of course had their own ideas about that and most of them sold a great deal of peatreek "under the counter".

With the universal popularity of the peatreek the gaugers were often spread very thinly indeed. As elsewhere, they were forced to rely on those most despicable of people - the informers. Sometimes, these were disgruntled or failed smugglers, sometimes people holding a personal grudge against a particular smuggler and sometimes even publicans. It was rare if not totally unknown for anyone to inform on the smugglers on principle. Throughout Scotland the use of the sma' still was not considered *really* criminal - it was seen as an expression of independence and a way of staying true to ancient tradition. As the most famous (though hardly successful) gauger of them all wrote,

> *Thae curst horse-leeches o the Excise*
> *Wha mak' the Whisky stills their prize!*
> *Haud up thy hand Deil, aince, twice, thrice*
> *There, sieze the blinkers,*
> *And bake them up in brunstane pies,*
> *For poor damned drinkers*

This was of course Robert Burns who spent a period as an Exciseman in Ayrshire. *Deil* is of course the Devil and *brunstane* simply means brimstone. Burns also wrote,

> *Freedom and Whisky gang thegither.*

One day in March in the mid-1820s, Henderson had received intelligence that a convoy of smugglers was on its way down Glen Shee from up near

Tales of Whisky and Smuggling

Braemar. It was said to be a convoy of a dozen ponies with a good deal of peatreek. The route they were taking would bring them down to the bridge over the Isla river at Bendochy, just north of Coupar Angus itself. It seemed clear that they were hoping Henderson and his gaugers would be out scouring the hillsides for bothies when they arrived. When he got the news, Henderson summoned his men from Blairgowrie and Alyth. By mid-morning next day, they were all hidden out of sight on the south side of the river close to the bridge.

The convoy of smugglers was coming down through Meiklour, wood having skirted wide round Blairgowrie. As usual, a couple of their number were ahead of the main body, keeping an eye out for the gaugers. Suddenly, one of the scouts, Donald Hardy, came running through the wood with a young lad by his side. He stopped and addressed William Gillespie, who was in charge of the convoy,

" William, this young lad here, he's Tom Speed's son and he says the gaugers are all lying in wait for us just the other side of the bridge."

Gillespie looked at the young lad, a fair-haired, lanky boy of about ten.

" So you are Tom's young boy are you?" he spoke slowly. Tom Speed was a local man who did a bit of distilling himself and Gillespie had known him for years. " What is your name then, lad?"

" Willie, Sir," replied the boy, proud as punch to be helping the Highland smugglers." Father saw the gaugers hiding and sent me to tell you there's about ten of them. He said that the Supervisor is with them. "

" Right. Ten of them you say," Gillespie said musingly, looking round as if to count his companions. With Hardy and the other scout there were still only eight of them and he didn't fancy a pitched battle so close to the town. He was remembering that the Scots Greys were still billeted there. By this time all the smugglers had gathered round him and had heard what the young lad had said.

" Can we not just be running straight through them?" put in Alexander Farquharson.

" Aye we could get the ponies going fast, straight at them and burst through," added his brother Charles.

" Aye and we might get past and lose half our *uisge beatha* too,' retorted Gillespie.

" We could double back and come round by Alyth," suggested Hardy.

" Aye we could, but the cursed gaugers obviously know we're coming so they would probably spot us once we're into the open country towards Meigle," Gillespie continued. " No, we'll have to think of some way of getting by them."

Suddenly there was a low laugh. It was old Sandy McGregor, a man who had been smuggling whisky for more than thirty years.

" I think I have it, "he said chuckling, " I think that we can get by the gaugers no bother at all."

Quickly he outlined his plan. Within minutes Hardy, old Sandy, Gillespie and the young lad headed off towards the nearby village of Ardblair. The remaining smugglers began to unload the whisky ankers from the line of ponies standing grazing quietly amongst the trees.

Not long after mid-day the gaugers, who were still hiding out of sight of the bridge heard the rumbling of a horse and cart on the Bendochy Bridge. Carefully lifting himself up from his position behind a ditch, Supervisor Henderson saw a man dressed entirely in black and wearing a tall black hat. The man was just coming off the bridge and down the road towards him. Behind him came a black-draped hearse, pulled by two black horses led by another man also dressed in black. The horses had high black plumes attached on their heads which bobbed as they walked along. Behind the hearse was a crowd of men, all of whom had strips of black cloth tied round the sleeves of their grey homespun jackets and round their hats. After the men was a small group of women, some in black and the others with black armbands.

" Stand up lads, show some respect," called Henderson, doffing his hat and nodding respectfully at the man at the front of the procession. On both sides of the road the gaugers appeared, doffing their hats and bowing their heads in respect as the cortege passed.

In complete silence, the funeral procession passed by and down the road into Coupar Angus. Within a few minutes all but the last of the women were out of sight.

" Right, men, back to your stations. Life goes on and we've smugglers to catch," he called out.

The funeral procession walked on through the small town and on along the road to Dundee. About half-a-mile on, the group turned off up a side road. The mourners calmly entered the courtyard of the farm just off the road and there was a blur of activity, interspersed with a good deal of laughter. Young Tom Speed had been sent ahead to his uncle's farm to arrange a horse and cart. Black armbands and hatcloths were stripped off and handed to the man who had been leading the hearse. The black cloth draped over the hearse was removed. There in place of the coffin were the barrels of peatreek that Gillespie and his friends were transporting. Within minutes Gillespie and Old Sandy were on their way south, having paid the Ardblair undertaker for the hire of his hearse and himself - with whisky that went back over the Bendochy Bridge in the hearse! The local women were each given a bladderskin of peatreek and the crowd dispersed. Over the next few hours they went back over the bridge at Bendochy in ones and twos and headed home. With them went the smugglers to wait for the return of

Tales of Whisky and Smuggling

Gillespie with their cash. The tired and bored gaugers sat throughout the afternoon still awaiting the smugglers' convoy.

By nightfall, Gillespie was angry and frustrated. Leaving a watch of two men on the bridge, he and the others went home. Over the next few months, the undertaker at Ardblair developed a nice sideline in ferrying ankers of whisky over the Isla, and the gaugers never noticed a thing. Old Sandy's reputation was much enhanced by this ploy and soon it was a standing joke among the smugglers how old Sandy McGregor was killing off the peaceful folk of Strathmore.

A few months after this famous episode, another convoy was heading towards Coupar Angus. It was late in the year and the days were short. The smugglers, from Glenisla, were anxious to get past the gaugers and on towards the Tay. Their destination was Invergowrie Bay, near Dundee, where they had arranged for some boats to help them shift their produce over to the thirsty folk of Fife. They were led by a canny smuggler from near Folda called Roderick MacIntosh. As usual, a man had been sent ahead to spy out the lie of the land and he met his fellows at Mudhall near Bendochy, where they intended fording the river. The gaugers had been keeping a watch on the bridge and they had decided to risk crossing the ford. The news from the scout was good. Not only was there no guard at the bridge but there was only one gauger in the town. The Supervisor and the other gaugers were off somewhere hounding some other poor smugglers.

" Ach well then, " said MacIntosh," let us just go straight through the town. One gauger will be no trouble to the four of us now will he?"

So the convoy of eight ponies was led back along to the Bendochy Bridge and over the river. As they came to the Causeway, the main street, they broke into a run and whooping and shouting ran with their ponies right through the centre of the wee town.

The sole gauger on duty was Willie Dickson. He was eating his dinner in the Strathmore Hotel when he heard the noise. Rushing out, he saw the smugglers coming down upon him.

" Stop in the name of the King, " he shouted, and jumped aside as the lead pony almost knocked him over. His only reply was a string of Gaelic which did not sound at all complimentary to his ears. Diving back into the Hotel he ran into the bar-room and shouted, "Who will give me a hand with these smugglers?"

There were nearly a dozen men in the room, farmers, smallholders and tradesmen. All looked at him.

"In the King's name, lend me some assistance to arrest these damned lawbreakers," he implored. Silence.

Turning, he ran back out into the main street. There ahead of him was the last of the ponies disappearing round the corner of the road to Dundee. He could still hear the smugglers yelling and shouting. He started running after them. Suddenly he stopped. What was that noise? He turned and there behind him in the doorway of the Strathmore Hotel were some of the men he had just asked for help. And all of them were laughing fit to burst. He looked around the street. There were at least a dozen other locals, one or two of whom were trying to keep a straight face. The rest were smiling and laughing at the sheer cheek of the smugglers.

Dickson was about to start calling them all a bunch of cowards and criminals, but then thought better of it. Scowling, he pushed through the crowd at the door of the hotel and returned to his meal. In the distance, the yelling and laughing of the smugglers was gently fading away.

Roderick MacIntosh was well known to the gaugers and when he heard of this blatant affront to the government, Supervisor Henderson decided to show the smuggler that he couldn't get away with this sort of behaviour. A few days later Henderson, Dickson and three other gaugers arrived at MacIntosh's house near Forter. To make sure of surprising the smuggler, they had made a wide detour, coming over the hills from Glen Prosen, ten miles to the east. The day had been getting mistier by the hour and their journey had been tortuous and hard.

The surprise wasn't total. As they rode down upon the steading they saw a woman run from the cottage with most of the pieces of a still on her back. She was a strong, good-looking woman in her thirties, and with her long black hair flowing behind her, she took off like a deer. Immediately giving chase up the track towards Carn an Fhidleir (The Fiddler's Cairn), they were soon almost on her.

" Stop woman! We are officers of His Majesty's Excise, put down that still. You are under arrest," called Henderson as they closed on the woman. She stopped and put down the still. But her next action was to fill her apron with stones from the side of the track.

"Come any closer and I will be braining you," she called. This was MacIntosh's wife Morag. Close to she was a handsome, flashing-eyed woman, but the way she held the stone in her hand looked as if she could indeed do as she threatened.

"Now, now, my good woman, you don't want to get in any more trouble than you are in already," Henderson started to say. He was about to go on when he noticed people coming towards them from all directions. Soon there were about twenty people gathered round. At once someone started shouting at the woman in Gaelic, telling her to run off into the gathering mist with the still. However the mounted gaugers had by now almost surrounded the woman and the crowd stayed back.

" Come on now, we don't want any trouble do we?" Henderson asked

Tales of Whisky and Smuggling

mildly, signalling to one of the gaugers to dismount and grab the still. Realising she was caught, Morag let her apron full of stones fall. The gaugers then rode back towards MacIntosh's cottage with Morag among them and the still on a horse being led by one of the gaugers.

At the door of the hut, MacIntosh stood with a gun in his hands. His long face was flushed with rage and his blue eyes were flashing. He was shouting incomprehensibly in Gaelic and looked dangerous. In a minute Henderson realised the man was drunk. He had been sampling a new batch of peatreek. That was why his wife had run off. MacIntosh was too befuddled with drink to make a run for it. The gaugers quietly drew pistols.

Henderson smiled. " There's no need for firearms Roderick, " he admonished. " We've caught you this time. You had better give over the gun before it's too late."

Swaying slightly, the smuggler looked around. Slowly he realised that there were several pistols pointing at him. A dismounted gauger had sneaked up close. He reached forward and snatched the gun and, checking it, found it wasn't loaded. Several of the gaugers then entered the house and found all of the rest of the still, bags of malt and a large quantity of low wines, as the first distilling of the barley was called.

The seriousness of the situation, and maybe the weather, which was rapidly getting colder soon sobered MacIntosh up. The gaugers soon found his greybeard, or bottle of whisky and several ankers more peatreek in an outhouse. Despite the state he was in MacIntosh realised that all the gaugers looked a bit damp, and made a suggestion.

"Och Mr. Henderson, you and your men look a bit cold and wet. I am sure a drop of my lovely whisky that you have all just confiscated would do you a bit of good now," he said slyly.

" That's a fine idea" said Dickson, " I for one am very cold Sir."

The other three gaugers murmured their assent.

" You are as cunning as a fox, Roderick MacIntosh. I do believe you are hoping to get us drunk and escape," said Henderson severely.

" Och no, no," the smuggler replied," you have caught me fair and square. I know I will have to come with you down to Coupar Angus. But you have me and you have my still," he sighed heavily," and you have my whisky. Do you need to be arresting Morag as well?"

Henderson looked long and hard at MacIntosh then spoke ," All right we'll take you and the whisky - your wife can go free. You know we'll have to destroy the still. It serves you right for what you did down in Coupar Angus."

" And what about a wee dram sir?" Dickson piped up.

" I doubt it will do us any harm. In this weather it will probably do us some good," the Supervisor said with a smile.

Soon the greybeard was being passed round. Poor MacIntosh could only watch as his precious still was smashed up, consoling himself with a nip or three from the big-bellied bottle the gaugers were happily passing round as they worked.

An hour or so later, MacIntosh said farewell to his beloved Morag. He might be away for a while and they both knew it. Then, with the ankers of whisky on MacIntosh's peat cart, and with Dickson driving it, the smuggler rode off with his captors. On the way back the weather got even colder and the smuggler's greybeard was filled, and emptied, at least twice more before the gaugers returned with their booty.

In less than a week MacIntosh was up in court, having spent the intervening time in prison.

When Henderson said that the gaugers had confiscated ten gallons of whisky, Macintosh spoke up.

" I am thinking it was nearer to eleven gallons your worship," he said to the Justice of the Peace, a gentleman who had in the past bought the odd anker of whisky from him. When the Justice heard that the entire company had got blazing drunk on the way down from Glenisla he could hardly keep a straight face. Henderson and the gaugers all made a great play of the fact that it had been a very cold, damp day. The people who had come to watch the proceedings hooted loudly at this.

After hearing all the evidence the Justice sternly said,

" There is no doubt that you are a hardened smuggler Roderick MacIntosh. However given that you have spent the last few days in prison and given the behaviour of the arresting officers," this with a stern look at the Supervisor, " I am going to fine you five shillings."

Henderson had smashed MacIntosh's still and put him out of business - for a little while. He could have asked for a much heavier fine or even for a prison sentence, but after that day coming down from Glenisla drinking the man's whisky, he was forced to admit the smuggler had got the better of him.

The magistrate that day was replaced soon after this by a man known to the people of the glens as Baillie John. Although by his own standards he was a fair man, the smugglers thought him hard. A man who drank little, he was a strong upholder of the law and, unlike his predecessor and many another magistrate of the time, he had little sympathy for the smugglers. To him the law was the law, and he had no hesitation in handing out jail sentences as well as stiff fines. If the fines he set weren't paid then he always made sure the culprits were jailed anyway.

One Saturday he was out walking along the banks of the Isla when he saw a man he recognised coming towards him.

Tales of Whisky and Smuggling

This was Donald MacRae from Strathardle, whom he had fined the previous month for being in possession of illicit spirits. He knew that Donald would be up before him the following Tuesday again, charged with running a still. The revenue men's case was weak in that they hadn't actually caught Donald red-handed but the bothy was very close to his croft and no one doubted it was his still they had located and destroyed.

" Good day Macrae," Baillie John said as the Highlander approached.

" Aye, it is a fine day indeed," Donald replied.

" Tell me, Donald, between ourselves, and out here away from the court. that was your still that Dickson and the others found wasn't it?" the magistrate asked.

" Och aye," the smuggler said back, " but they have no proof at all."

" What," demanded the Baillie," are you telling me you intend getting off by giving a false oath?"

Nodding, Donald spoke," Aye that I will. There is mercy in Heaven with the Lord Almighty but there's none with Baillie John. Good Day Baillie."

As the red-headed smuggler walked away, the Baillie turned and looked after him, a strange look on his face. Anyone seeing him at that moment might have thought it was a look of doubt, but the smugglers of the hills above Strathmore would never have believed that!

So the Tuesday came around and Donald was charged with running an illicit still and defrauding the Government of its due revenue.

Baillie John looked directly at McRae. " Will you swear on oath that you are not guilty as charged here, MacRae?" he demanded sternly.

Looking the Baillie straight in the eyes, Donald answered, "Yes I will swear that. I am not guilty."

He looked confident but inside the smuggler was knotted up with fear. What would Baillie John do to him? The man knew he was guilty, didn't he?

The courtroom was deathly quiet as the Baillie stared at the man in the dock. Then after what seemed an age to MacRae, he spoke, " I find the defendant not guilty. Go home, you rascal, and make sure I never see your face in this court again. If I do, it will go very badly for you."

As the delighted MacRae turned to leave the dock the magistrate added,

"And tell your friends in the smuggling trade that there's mercy with Baillie John as well as with the Almighty."

Donald never lost his enjoyment of a glass or two of peatreek but from that time on he never again ran a still. And if Baillie John ever figured out who left the twenty-pound salmon on his doorstep early in the morning three days later, he never said.

A few years earlier there, had been an incident involving Superintendent

Henderson and his men with a bunch of smugglers that had resulted in jail terms for quite a few of the peatreek men. One of the gaugers in Meigle, a man from the Borders called Gray, was keeping an eye on a local carter called Wright who lived at Kirkinch at the foot of Kinpurney Hill in the Sidlaws, notable for an imitation ruined castle on its summit. This had been built in the late eighteenth century to allow a local landowner to indulge his passion for astronomical observations.

Gray believed that the carter was using his legitimate business as a cover for transporting peatreek, and regularly watched his home at Kirkinch. One evening in December, hiding in the bracken on the slopes of Kinpurney, well wrapped up in a blanket, he saw Wright arriving from the north with a couple of men on the cart with him. It was beginning to get dark but Gray recognised one of the men as Charles Grant, a notorious smuggler from faraway Donside. Through his spyglass he saw the three men dismount and pull out a barrel from underneath the tarpaulin on the back of the cart. They then carried the barrel into Wright's house.

At once, Gray headed into the nearby village of Newytle where he had left his horse with the local butcher. Within minutes he was riding hard for Coupar Angus to inform the Supervisor. On hearing the news, Henderson laid his plans and the following morning at seven o'clock he, Gray and two other gaugers, Sutherland and Flowerden headed off to Kirkinch.

The first Wright knew of the gaugers' presence was a loud hammering on his front door. On opening the door he was brushed aside as Henderson and Gray thrust their way into the house.

"We have reason to believe you have illicit spirits here, Wright and we are conducting a search in the King's name," Henderson said, thrusting his face close to Wright's. At once the two of them began to search the house while outside the other pair of gaugers searched the outhouses and stables.

In minutes Gray located a "graybeard", a five-gallon earthenware crock, in the meal chest in the kitchen.

"Right then," Henderson said with a smile, " you are under arrest. It will go better if you tell us where the rest is."

"I don't know what you are talking about," mumbled Wright.

At that point Sutherland and Flowerden came into the cottage kitchen.

"We can't see anything right off, Mr. Henderson," Sutherland reported.

" Well you'll just have to look harder then, off you go," replied the Supervisor.

" Wait a minute," Gray suddenly shouted, falling to his knees a couple of feet in front of the meal chest. He drew a clasp knife from his coat pocket and, opening it, inserted the blade between two flagstones. One of them moved and within seconds the gauger had his fingers under the edge of the stone. He lifted it up. There was a dark hole in the floor with the top of a ladder clearly visible.

" Watch him Sutherland," barked Henderson, as he noticed Wright tense. "Flowerden fetch over that lantern there by the window and we'll see what Mr. Wright is keeping in this handy little cellar."

The lantern was lit and by its light they could clearly see more than a couple of dozen barrels in the room below. They had obviously discovered a big distribution ring. Henderson smiled, stood up from looking into the cellar and turned to Wright. Just as he was about to speak there was a commotion at the door.

In burst Charles Grant, followed by James McPherson and Peter McKay, all hardened smugglers from up north, who had spent the night with another friend close by. The small kitchen was now jampacked and Gray was in danger of being pushed into the cellar. Outside there was the noise of running feet as others arrived. Things looked bleak for the gaugers. They had thought they would be dealing with only one or two men and now the numbers were even, with more smugglers, or at least their supporters, outside in the yard.

" You will be leaving our *uisge beatha* alone or it will be the worse for you," threatened Grant.

" You are meddling with an Officer of the King in the rightful performance of his duties," riposted Henderson, cursing that his pistols were still in their holsters on his horse's saddle outside. " I must warn you that you are all in serious trouble. Very serious trouble indeed. If you have any sense you will leave us to get on with our duty and make yourselves scarce."

Grant, who was pressed close against the Supervisor, laughed in his face. Just then Peter McKay spoke up.

" We are not wanting to have any trouble here. I think I know what we should do," he said in a reasonable manner. All eyes turned to him.

"Now we all know that the officers have caught us here, fair and square. Wheesht now Charlie let me have my say," he said to Grant. " Now we have come a long way with our whisky - and it took us a lot of work making it. You can appreciate that sir, can you not," he continued, addressing Henderson, obviously the Supervisor, with his red coat.

" You are breaking the law, my man and it is my duty to uphold the Excise laws here," Henderson spat angrily. There was a murmur from the crowd at the door and the smugglers in the kitchen pressed forward a little.

" Now, now that is as may be, but you can see that there is no way we are going to let you take the whisky. Use your eyes man, there are too many of us," the Highlander went on. " Now if we let you have the greybeard there and let you go, we could just move our peatreek along and out of your district right away. That way you would not be going back empty-handed."

128

Henderson looked around the press of bodies in the kitchen and out of the door where there seemed to be at least eight or nine men gathered. It was a tricky situation. He obviously couldn't take the whisky by force against these odds. If he tried, he and his men would suffer injuries, maybe severe injuries. This smuggler called Charlie looked extremely dangerous. The carter, Wright would be stopped from all future ferrying of peatreek now that the gaugers knew of his activities. Still, a greybeard wasn't enough for the trouble he had gone to. Henderson knew the odds were stacked against him but he was no coward.

" All right, I can see some sense in what you say," he began. Then, choosing his words carefully he went on, " But I will need to take at least three barrels to make it worth our while."

Grant exploded into a stream of Gaelic and the gaugers were pushed back again. Gray was precariously balanced over the hole to the cellar and struggling hard to avoid falling.

" Now, now, " shouted McKay, " calm down Charlie, we will work it out, don't you worry."

Within a few minutes a bargain was struck. The smugglers would let the gaugers ride off with the greybeard and one barrel, and the gaugers would not return for at least two hours. They would be given the loan of a horse which Henderson had agreed could be collected later in Coupar Angus. Unhappily, but realising he had to make the best of a bad job, Henderson had agreed. His men were relieved. They knew they would have suffered badly if Henderson had not agreed to the bargain suggested by McKay.

As they rode off towards Coupar Angus, the gaugers were quite happy with the way things had turned out, but Henderson was furious. However, he had given his word, so the four Excise officers were walking their horses and had just passed Fullarton, about a mile up the road, when the situation changed again.

The hot-headed Charlie Grant had no intention of giving up any of the whisky. He and James McPherson had sneaked up on the gaugers with some of the younger locals. They had come through the woods on either side of the road. As soon as they rushed from the woods it was obvious they had a plan worked out. The gaugers were taken totally by surprise. They were pulled from their horses and the horses were immediately hit with sticks and galloped off up the road. Grant grabbed the pony with the whisky and as the gaugers were held down on the road by MacPherson and the others he made off quickly. As soon as he was a little way off, the men holding the gaugers down let them go and ran off in different directions through the wood. By the time they were on their feet there was little point in chasing after them. The whole thing had taken no more than a couple of minutes. Henderson was beside himself with anger. He was so incensed he couldn't speak. There

129

was no way he would let this affront to his position and his pride pass.

As soon as they got back to Coupar Angus a couple of hours later, he swore out warrants against the smugglers. Though it was only Grant and MacPherson who had gone back on the bargain, all would pay. Then he summoned the dragoons and headed back to Kirkinch. The whisky of course was gone, but two dragoons were left to arrest Wright as soon as he returned. Within days he was sentenced to six months for supplying peatreek.

It took Henderson a few months to find out exactly who all the smugglers were, but in time he had his revenge. Grant, MacPherson, MacKay and Stewart were all found guilty of the crime of *deforcement* - the forcible preventing of an officer of the law from the execution of his office. They were all jailed for nine months. Grant in particular probably spent much of his sentence regretting not going along with the diplomatic McKay's well worked bargain.

Auld Jean o' Bladder Ha'

Whether the whisky supplied to the towns and villages of Scotland came from local sma' stills or from faraway Highland glens, the last leg of its journey was the most difficult. The gaugers always kept an eye out for whisky coming into the towns and cities. The Highland convoys would generally stop a few miles short of their destination and transfer the peatreek from the five or ten gallon barrels into smaller receptacles. They often stopped at springs or wells, places of long-term significance for the local people. Generally the couriers at this stage were women and there were many tricks used. Barrels small enough to be hidden under skirts, if gaugers were about, milk-pails and churns with false bottoms and custom-made tin flasks of all shapes and sizes were all common. The preferred method in many areas, however was bladder-skins. Depending on which animal they came from, these came in many sizes and had the great advantage of being flexible.

A well known smuggler who regularly visited Dundee put the bladders to good effect. His name was Geordie Fleming, a quiet and pleasant man from just outside the town. Geordie was easily spotted in a crowd for from quite a young age he had sported an unusually tall hat. This was looked on as a harmless eccentricity and caused no comment. Under the hat Geordie habitually had a bladder-skin full of his own whisky which he delivered to his customers with no fear of detection, a few pints at a time.

It wasn't just the handiness of the bladders that made them popular. It was believed by many that whisky that was transported by bladder skin was stronger and better then any other. The sma' stills could never produce pure alcohol - there was always a large percentage of water. It seems that by being kept in a bladder-skin and warmed up the peatreek was subjected to Soemmering's process. This process allowed a good deal of the water to escape through the pores of the membrane of the bladder while the whisky remained. As the bladder-skins were generally kept close to the body under the clothes, this ensured the whisky increased in strength. Or so it was generally believed.

The bladders were of course easy to hide and were often transported under women's skirts. The gaugers of course were aware of this and their searching of women was often coarse indeed. There were many of the women smugglers who were more than a match for the gaugers. One of these was an elderly, buxom lady called Jean Anderson from just outside Dundee, who made and smuggled her own whisky. Jean shifted virtually all her whisky by bladder. In fact she was so fond of using them that there were bladders hanging up on all the walls of her cottage to the north of the town. The humble dwelling was known by friends, neighbours and customers as Bladder Ha'.

Jean had been widowed when she was still quite young and had supported herself for years by her skill at making peatreek. She had plenty of regular customers in the nearby city and could have sold twice as much as she did. Even as she grew into middle age and beyond she still convoyed her own wares into her customers. The fame of her peatreek spread in time to the gaugers of course and over the years Auld Jean o' Bladder Ha' had many run-ins with the men of the Excise. And in all of these instances, the wily smuggler had the best of matters.

When she was still a young woman and making whisky with her husband, Jean had her first serious encounter with a gauger. She was a fine looking woman with long golden-red hair, beautiful, big, blue eyes and a full, shapely figure. One cold March evening she was walking through the Emmock woods to a customer at Trottick just north of Dundee. Under her voluminous dress she had three bladder skins of peatreek - about nine or ten pints in all. As she walked through the woods she was startled as a man jumped out in front of her from behind a tree.

" Aha my lass. Would you be one of these smugglers then?' the man said, looking her up and down. " I am Revenue Officer Stewart and I will have to search you,' he went on, with a lascivious smile. Looking at him, at his hooked nose, deep-set eyes, greying beard and thin lips, Jean realised that this was Geordie Stewart the gauger, a man well known for accosting young women in the name of searching them for bladders of whisky. He was a foul creature and never attempted to stop male smugglers unless with other gaugers. He was loathed by everyone in the district.

Dropping her eyes, Jean said shyly, " Oh, sir you startled me, but I am no smuggler. I am just going down to Trottick to pick up my wee bairnie from my mother."

"That's as may be," leered the gauger, coming closer," but it is my duty to search you in the King's name. So just you stand still while I have a wee look."

Coming right up to her, the gauger bent down and grabbed her skirts to lift them right up. Jean was ready for him. As he moved, so did she. In one fluid movement she hiked her skirts up at the back, swung up one of the bladders tied round her waist and brought it down over the man's head. The bladder burst. The whisky poured over Stewart's head and into his eyes. Screaming, he stood up clutching at his eyes. Jean stepped back. Almost totally blinded, the roaring gauger stumbled to his knees. Jean didn't move."My eyes, my eyes! You've blinded me you devil! My eyes, my eyes," the gauger roared. Then, getting to his feet, he ran towards Trottick. Jean followed on behind.

A hundred yards or so down the road crossed the Dighty Water. Stewart stumbled down the road and reaching the old stone bridge left the road and ran into the water. Kneeling there in the ice-cold burn he began splashing water in his eyes. Jean stopped momentarily on the bridge to look at the moaning figure in the stream below before walking calmly on to deliver her peatreek. After delivering her goods Jean went carefully home by a roundabout route. After that she was never bothered by Stewart again. In fact he soon turned to other work, becoming a gamekeeper on an estate near Forfar.

Even if one gauger retired there was always another and down through the years Jean became adept at avoiding the government's representatives. She was greatly helped in this by the network of friends and customers she had in the area.

Many years later she had another problem on the same bit of road. She was calmly heading towards home leading her sheltie, or pony, laden with bags of malt one clear, late October night. The possession of more than a small amount of malt was in itself an infringement of the excise laws. The air was crisp, the stars shone brightly in the cloudless sky and Jean was thinking of the impending birth of a baby to one of her nieces. She would have to make sure she had plenty of whisky for the family to "wet the bairns' head", as the celebratory drinking at a birth was (and still is) known. She was coming up the tree-lined path through the Emmock woods just where it entered a cutting, and for once in her life wasn't paying attention to her surroundings.

Suddenly a gauger was there on the road. " Right, Mistress Anderson. " he said with satisfaction. " Let me have the pony. I am confiscating that malt."

This was a gauger called McLaughlin, a stout, red-haired man with an open, florid countenance. He appeared to be in his late twenties. Like most of

133

his colleagues, he knew of Jean Anderson's activities and had long wanted to catch her. Reaching out, he tore the reins of the pony from her hand. Jean looked at him. Did this upstart gauger think he could have her malt just like that? Well then, she thought, he's in for a shock.

Without a change in her expression Jean, by now well into her fifties, launched herself at McLaughlin. Down they both fell. The gauger was momentarily stunned by this direct approach and Jean gave him a couple of socks to the jaw. He pulled himself together and they rolled about on the road for a couple of minutes each trying to get the upper hand. Jean realised she had little chance of getting the better of this young, strong man. Tearing herself from his grasp she got to her feet and ran off back towards Trottick.

Getting to his feet and shaking his head in wonder at the woman's assault, the gauger got hold of the pony and headed in the same direction, dusting off his clothes as he went. At least he had the malt, and he would have yet another story to tell the other gaugers about the redoubtable Jean Anderson. He began to laugh, admiring the woman's spirit and bravery. What he didn't know was that Jean, as wily as ever, had not given up the fight.

A few minutes after the scuffle the door of the inn at Mains of Trottick flew open. There in the door stood the bedraggled and flustered figure of a woman in her fifties, dressed in the black clothes of a widow. The men in the bar turned to stare. Most of them knew at once who it was. One of the men sitting by the fire was a blacksmith, a newcomer to the village. His name was Willie Govan and seeing this distressed woman he spoke out.

" What ails you mistress. Are you in some trouble?" he asked, getting up from his seat. He was a giant of a man and seemed to fill the small room as he rose.

" I have just been attacked in the woods by a robber," Jean panted, breathless from running to the inn. " He has taken my pony and my goods, that I was taking home."

"Good Lord above, what kind of scoundrel would attack a poor widow?" roared the blacksmith. " Just you get your breath back and then lead me to where you were attacked Mistress. I'll soon find him and teach the blackguard not to attack defenceless ladies. Who'll come with me?"

This question was met by a chorus of " I will " and "Me too", and a few minutes later the entire company streamed out of the inn door and off towards the Emmock woods. Most of them realised what had happened and were keen to put one over on the Exciseman but Govan and one or two others were only aware that they were after a ruthless scoundrel who preyed on old women.

McLaughlin was heading up the hill towards Dundee just the other side of the village when the crowd came from the inn.

Auld Jean o' Bladder Ha'

"There he is," a cry went up and the gauger turned. There, streaming towards him, was a band of about twenty men lead by a veritable giant. He didn't wait to find out what was happening. Dropping the pony's reins he took off as fast as he could run. Govan came up and, taking the pony's reins handed them to one of his companions, saying, " Here, you take this back to that poor woman. I'm going after that scoundrel."

Luckily for the gauger, fear gave him added speed and he managed to keep well ahead of Govan and the three or four young lads who went with him, in the hope of seeing the gauger get a thumping. It wasn't long before Govan realised they weren't going to catch the supposed robber and decided to return to the inn. MacLaughlin didn't stop running until he reached the city. He had no intention of returning that night.

Back at the inn, Jean was relaxing with a glass of her own peatreek from the landlord's supply when the smith returned. He insisted on walking her the couple of miles home when she was ready to go.

When they got back to her home, Jean went into her cottage, telling the big blacksmith to wait a minute. It wasn't until she came back out and handed him a bladder of the finest peatreek that Govan realised what had happened. He saw the humour of the situation and, once he had drunk the contents of the bladder, became a regular customer of the Mistress o' Bladder Ha'.

The following year in late September, Jean got a request from an old friend. His daughter was getting married and he wanted nothing but the best for her great day. So he would like Jean to supply the whisky and would she please attend the wedding. It was a big order and Jean was pleased to get the invitation. There was only one problem. The gaugers were highly active at the time and many smugglers had been arrested.

It had all started a few weeks before, when the Supervisor from Coupar Angus, Mr. Henderson, had been visiting his colleagues in Dundee. He was walking through the centre of the bustling city to the office of the Collector of Excise in Barrack Street when he saw a man he recognised. The man was walking up the steps to the whisky store of the then Lord Provost with a sack on his back.

" Hey, you, John Carnegie, what have you got in that sack?" shouted Henderson as he walked towards the man.

"Potatoes," replied Carnegie, recognising the Supervisor and looking a little sheepish.

" Well let me just have a look," Henderson demanded, coming up the stairs.

The sack contained a twenty-pint anker of whisky and Henderson confiscated it on the spot. As it had been confiscated outside his whisky

Tales of Whisky and Smuggling

store, the Lord Provost got off with a warning. However such blatant flouting of the law angered the Supervisor. So after a long talk with the Collector of Excise, Robert Sinclair, he decided to make an extra special effort against the smugglers in the area. In this they were greatly helped by the collector's clerk, Mungo Park, a descendant of the great explorer. Gaugers were brought in from all over Angus and Perthshire and the people of the Dundee area were soon cursing the drought of whisky caused by all this activity.

An old friend of Jean's, Peter Donnachie, was soon caught near Downfield. He was taking an anker of peatreek in his cart under a covering of straw when stopped by the gaugers. He was taken off to the official headquarters of the Excise in Barrack Street, a gauger leading his horse and cart with Peter walking alongside. Peter's daughter Anne, a smart and bonny lass of eighteen, had seen what had happened. Running off, she found one of her friends and they followed the cart along the road to Dundee. Quickly, the two girls formed a plan. Anne's friend Lizzie ran on ahead, leaving the main road to get ahead of the cart.

As she walked back up the road the bonny young lass smiled at the gauger. " Good afternoon," he said, " it's a fine day for a stroll"

Lizzie nodded, and, still smiling at the gauger, looked quizically at Peter.

"Och he's one of the smugglers I've just caught," the gauger smugly said.

Giggling, Lizzie looked down and walked on, giving Peter a sly wink as she passed.

Turning to look at the girl as she walked off the gauger gave a sigh and said, " Come on Peter, let's get going. It's a shame there' s no time to get to know that bonny lass."

" Aye, she's a bonny wee thing right enough,' replied Peter, " but there's a lot o' bonny lasses round about here. Are there as many where you come from? Where is it you're from anyway?"

Soon Peter had the gauger deep in conversation. Lizzie walked up the road a bit to meet Anne then quietly they followed the horse, cart and two men, keeping to the fields at the edge of the road. Soon they had caught up on the cart. Peter and the gauger were still conversing away. The two lassies ran out and between them lifted the anker cleanly off the cart. The gauger didn't see a thing. Hiding it safely nearby for later, Anne thanked Lizzie then ran on to catch up with her father.

She caught up with him in Dundee just as he arrived at Barrack Street and the absence of the anker was discovered.

As she approached and greeted her father, the gauger suspiciously demanded, " Do you ken anything about this missing anker of whisky?"

The absolute picture of innocence, Anne looked at him with her big brown eyes and said, " As long as it was my father's property I looked after it, but when it belonged to you and the government I had nothing to do with it." With the proof gone, Peter had to be released and later that day he delivered his whisky, a little late but none the less welcome for that.

Out in her cottage near the Claverhouse bleachfields Jean realised that it would be difficult getting the whisky through to the wedding. But one way or another she was determined to find a way. If she couldn't, being a guest at the wedding herself, she too would be forced to drink the commercial spirits that she and her contemporaries so despised. Suddenly she had it - of course - she was to be a guest at the wedding. Laughing to herself she went to a cupboard and opened it. There at the bottom of the press, as she called it, was a gift she had been given a few years ago from the wife of a local Justice of the Peace. He had been a good customer and she had become friendly with his wife. One day the woman had given her a splendid gold and silver coloured ball-gown that had belonged to her recently married daughter. As the daughter was about her size, Jean had accepted the dress, knowing that there would be little chance for her to wear such an item of clothing. But it would be perfect for the wedding in Dundee.

The day of the wedding dawned bright and fair. Late in the morning the people on the outskirts of Dundee were the first to see Jean dressed for her wedding. As she came through the streets on her old pony she looked remarkable. The ball-gown nearly hid the poor pony entirely. All that could be seen were its head and its hooves. The style was not that long out of fashion but there was something hilarious about this elderly country wife, with her weather-beaten features, sitting on the back of a Highland sheltie kitted out like a lady of fashion. There were a few sarcastic comments about mutton dressed as lamb and quite a few children openly laughed but Jean rode on, all smiles, waving regally at the passers-by.

At last she came to the tenement building in the Overgate where the wedding was being held. Passing through into the courtyard of the big building she was greeted by an expectant throng of people coming out of the bride's house.

" It's Auld Jean, " the cry went up and the young, (and not-so-young) men clustered round to help her from her horse. With a couple of lads keeping an eye open out in the street on the off chance of a gauger passing by, the others removed the bladders hanging from the saddle of the wee pony. Jean was escorted in grand style up the stairs by the bride's father. Now that the necessary supplies had arrived, the celebrations could really begin.

Tales of Whisky and Smuggling

It was a fine wedding, Jean's peatreek making sure that the singing and dancing was truly spirited. As she herself said to a friend a few days later, "It's just as well my old pony knows the way home. It was probably the dancing but I fell asleep on the way home. Whisky? Och yes I had a few glasses but it was the dancing that tired me out."

Jean kept on making the peatreek for many years, but the government eventually did put her out of business. In 1834 a new law was passed which empowered the courts to fine landlords on whose lands whisky was found being made. This was the death knell for many smugglers, as the Lairds were quite prepared to turn a blind eye only as long as it didn't cost them. Hit them in the pocket and they would always respond. So Jean was told to stop making whisky if she wanted to stay in her cottage. After a virtual lifetime in the peatreek trade her reaction to this command was philosophical.

She told her neighbours, "Och I've had a good run. I'm getting too old for it anyway and I've enough stuff hidden away around the cottage to see me out. *Slainte!*"

The Bothy Tycoon

John Munro of Invergordon was known as *John Dearg* - Red John. This naming of people after the colour of their hair was and is, common practice among the Gaelic-speaking peoples of Scotland. In areas where nearly everyone has the same surname and there aren't enough first names to go round, it makes sense to give people nicknames to tell them from each other. Sometimes nicknames would refer to hair-colouring or physical size, sometimes to aspects of character and sometimes to particular occupations or even places of residence. There were many Munros in Easter Ross but John Dearg was one of the best known. Although he lived in Invergordon he was heavily involved in the peatreek industry throughout the area. In fact he was almost a bothy tycoon - he had bothies all over the area and had a wide ranging distribution network for his own and others' whisky. His profession of ship's chandler gave him a perfect front for his illegal activities, though he never had even a drop of peatreek near his shop in Invergordon. Invergordon was a thriving fishing port and its situation on the Cromarty Firth - nowadays utilised by the North Sea oil industry - made it ideal for John's activities.

Whisky was made in the glens of Ben Tarsuinn and Ben Wyvis, in sea-caves on the the Nigg peninsula and all over the Black Isle. Much of this peatreek was destined to be distributed by John Dearg. He used fishing-boats, carts, hearses and a host of other forms of transport to bring the peatreek into Invergordon then to send it on its way south. He had customers in Inverness, all along the coast of the Moray Firth and much further south.

He was a clever, even devious man, known for driving a hard bargain and possessed of a truly Highland sense of honour. His word was his bond.

Some of the bothies he set up himself were very models of subterfuge. One, near Dalmore was built directly under the end of a cottage, the smoke from the peatreek-making being emitted through the cottage's lum or chimney. A favourite trick of John's was to build a bothy underground just outside a *clachan* or village. The lum of a bothy like this was simply a hole in the roof. If the gaugers were about, a large iron pot full of washing would be placed over the opening and one or two local ladies would stand over it, turning the washing with sticks. From even quite close up this would look like everyday domestic activity.

Despite the great ingenuity shown, there were still instances of the gaugers catching smugglers red-handed. One of John Dearg's regular suppliers was Ewan Urquhart who lived at Foulis Mains overlooking the Cromarty Firth and the Black Isle. He was busy one day in his barn putting a batch of malt into bags ready for taking to the kiln for drying. His daughter Moll was giving him a hand. They were busy at this when a gauger from Inverness crept up on the barn. Finding the barn-door securely locked he moved to a small window. Pulling out the window, frame and all he stuck his head through the opening. Now he was a fit, young man and his greatest pride was his beard which was thick, black and came half-way down his chest. As soon as she saw this hirsute Exciseman stick his head through the window hole, Moll sprang forward. She grabbed him by his long beard and held him fast.

At once Ewan cried, " Cum greim cruaidh air a bheist (Keep a hard grip of the beast) in Gaelic; then in English," Och, let go the poor gentleman's beard Moll."

Quickly bagging the last of his malt the smuggler kept shouting the two phrases turn about. The poor gauger couldn't pull away from Moll's grip. The constant shouting and the tears springing to his eyes from the tugging at his beard were confusing to say the least. He kept bellowing. " Let me go woman, let me go in the name of the King," but Moll hung grimly on. As soon as he had the bags filled, Ewan proceeded to take them out of the barn and hide them in the heather behind the house, still shouting to Moll as he did so. With the gauger's yells and Ewan's alternate instructions there was a terrible racket, made worse by Ewan's two dogs snarling and yelping at the gauger's behind.

It only took a few minutes to hide the malt, and as he came back to the barn Ewan called to Moll to let the gauger go. At her father's word she did so and the poor struggling gauger fell back on one of the dogs. The dog yelped and nipped the gauger's left buttock. The gauger yelled and leapt to his feet. The smuggler stood at the barn door. Behind him appeared his daughter.

The dogs bared their teeth. Tears streaming from his eyes and blood from his punctured backside, the gauger had had enough. Bellowing with rage and fear he ran off, the dogs nipping at his heels. Behind him father and daughter burst into laughter as he fled.

When he heard the story, John Munro had a good laugh. He was always greatly pleased at putting one over on the government men. Not longer after though he was caught napping by the gaugers himself.

John had a big two-storied house in the centre of Invergordon, where he lived with his wife, son and daughter, his widowed mother and a couple of maiden aunts of his wife. He was happy to use his wealth to support his extended family and all of them at one time or another helped him in his illegal activities. Many cousins too had been set up in whisky-making in the surrounding area by the canny John Dearg. His house had massive cellars where he stored the large amounts of peatreek he so regularly sent south. The entrance to the cellar was through a trap door in the drawing room, under a carpet.

Because of the extent of his business, John had arrangements with several crofters in outlying villages, who would send word if there was any sign of gaugers approaching.

One evening he was in the kitchen, calmly going over the books of his illicit business. A travelling tailor, Tam Tyler, was sitting cross-legged on the kitchen table, sewing the jacket of a new suit for John. It was common for tailors in country districts to move from house to house, getting board and lodging while they made up any clothes that were needed. They would then receive an agreed price. John Dearg was a good customer of Tyler's but because the standard of food and drink in his house was so high he always drove a hard bargain on price with the tailor.

John was happy. His cellars were full of ankers of peatreek, a boat was ready and waiting in the harbour and in a few minutes he would have yet another consignment under way. He sighed contentedly. Things were going well indeed.

Suddenly, there was a hammering at the door and a dishevelled figure burst in. It was Willie Johnston, the skipper of the boat John was using to ship his consignment.

" Quick John! " he burst out. " It's the gaugers, they're in the town - a good dozen of them"

"What?" cried John," Why didn't I get word?"

" The devils came in on a Buckie fishing boat from Inverness," spat Johnston. " I know the man who has that boat and I'll. . ."

"Never mind that," thundered John. " How close are they?"

"Well they seem to be stopping at a few houses, but they've split up so they'll be here in minutes," replied the fisherman.

"Right," John said decisively. " Tyler would you like to earn a boll of malt?" This was three hundred pounds weight, and worth a good few pounds. John had hardly any cash, having paid for all the contents of the cellar.

Tyler didn't hesitate," What do you want me to do?" he asked.

" Go through to the drawing room and tell Mrs Munro to lay you out on the big table," John spoke rapidly, turning to Johnston and continuing, " Willie, get as many men as you can, keep them out of sight till I get rid of these damned government flunkies. We'll have to shift the lot as quick as we can. Get a couple of laddies to scout the back gardens and go that way to the harbour. "

By now the house was astir as the women began to arrange matters in the front room. Johnson went out of the back door towards the harbour to organise the removal of the whisky. John went to the drawing room.

Soon the big dining table was securely over the trap door. Lying on it was Tyler, his jaw bound up with a snow-white linen cloth, a sheet of the same pristine softness draped over him and a plate of salt lying on his stomach. At his head and feet candles were burning. Around the table all the womenfolk apart from John's wife were kneeling. Just as she handed her husband the family Bible, a massive volume bound with leather and trimmed with brass, there was a tremendous knocking at the front door.

"Open up in the King's Name," a voice thundered. The women began muttering prayers and, picking up a candle, John was about to turn to the door when there was a whisper.

"Two bolls of malt," the tailor muttered through his teeth.

Hesitating slightly, John nodded and went to the door.

There was another hammering on the door.

"Open up in there I say," the voice came again.

John unbolted the door and swung it open.

There was a stout, middle-aged man in a Supervisor's red coat and behind him were three other men. All were carrying swords and the candlelight glinted off the pistols in the Supervisor's belt. This was Alexander Grahame, Supervisor of Excise at Inverness and without doubt the organiser of this sneaking, night-time invasion by the gaugers.

" Mr. Grahame," John spoke slowly and sombrely, " you have come to a house of mourning, but in you come, in you come," he went on, stepping aside to let the four men enter the house. Grahame's eyes went to the big Bible clutched under Munro's arm.

" Follow me," the smuggler spoke, and led the gaugers into the drawing room.

There they saw a body laid out in traditional fashion in the middle of the room, surrounded by weeping and praying women.

" You have come upon us at a sad time indeed. This is my only brother Thomas laid out before you." He reached down and laid his hand on his mother's shoulder," Never fear mother, he has gone to a far better place. Oh Thomas, Thomas" he stuttered, a catch in his throat.

Grahame was embarrassed. Only a few minutes ago he had been intent on turning the whole house upside down. He was damned sure that Munro was one of the people responsible for the shipments of peatreek that he knew were landing regularly on the Moray coast. But how could he interrupt this tragic family scene? Just at that moment John's mother let out a heavy groan and collapsed on the floor. At once the other women clustered round.

"Take her to her room," John ordered. " Out of the way, out of the way. Let my mother pass,' he said to the gaugers. At once they backed out into the lobby of the house and as the other women helped Mrs. Munro from the drawing-room Grahame waved his men back out of the still-open door.

" I am truly sorry to disturb you at this tragic time. You have my condolences in your loss," he said to Munro as he too backed out of the door, pulling it closed behind him.

The moment the door closed there was another burst of activity. John, his wife and daughter went into the drawing-room. Tyler leapt from the table and helped Munro move it against the wall. John's wife and daughter rolled up the carpet. His mother went to the back door and opened it. In came Johnston with half-a-dozen men. They went into the drawing-room just as John Dearg raised the trapdoor. Grabbing a candle, he descended the steps to the cellar followed by Johnston and the others. More men arrived through the back door.

With the women watching through the curtains, the barrels of whisky, some sixty odd of them, were ferried out of the kitchen door and taken through the adjoining gardens towards the harbour.

No-one spoke. The occasional "wheesht" stopped the convoy of anker-laden smugglers as one of the look-outs saw the gaugers moving from house to house. Silently, the precious cargo was moved through gardens and back lanes to the waiting vessel. With a whole gang of boys watching for the gaugers, by ones and twos the barrels crossed the wide area adjoining the harbour and were put on board Johnston's boat.

In the town Grahame was going about his business.

He had an extensive list of men he thought were involved in large-scale smuggling. His informants had told him that there was a shipment ready to go, but house after house proved empty of all but the odd flagon or two of peatreek. The owners were relieved of these but there was no point in bringing them to trial for such trifling amounts. Grahame was after much bigger fish. He had been sure that John Munro was one of the ringleaders but not even a smuggler would continue his illicit business with his brother laid out in the house. There must be others who were running the whisky. Still he had been so sure. He had just conducted a fruitless search of the house of a local butcher, Joseph Findlay, when he asked,"When exactly did John Dearg's brother die?"

Findlay looked at the Supervisor as if he was daft.

"John Dearg has three sisters that I know of, but he has no brother at all," the butcher replied.

" The devious dog," bellowed Grahame to his men. "Back to Munro's house. Hurry, hurry."

Pulling a whistle from his pocket he blew furiously, summoning the other two groups of gaugers. They ran back through the streets, one of the other groups meeting them just as they got to Munro's door.

" Break in that door," the furious Supervisor roared.

The door was promptly smashed down. The gaugers rushed into the house. Gahame ran to the kitchen. Others ran to the drawing room. There in the flickering candle light the Supervisor saw a tailor sitting cross-legged on the table, busily sewing. Tyler looked up and quietly said, " If you are looking for John Dearg, sir, he has just stepped out with Mrs. Munro, but I'm sure he won't be long."

In the drawing-room three elderly women, John's mother included, were sitting around the table sipping tea. Try as the gaugers might they could get no sense from them. None of the government men had the Gaelic and none of the ladies had the English, the tailor explained.

" Search the house! " Grahame shouted angrily.

" Is there any point in that sir?" asked one of his men. " If Munro's gone so is the whisky, don't you think?"

Furiously Grahame glared at him. Of course the man was right.

" Quickly, to the harbour. That's where they'll have gone. We'll have them yet," he cried.

As the armed gaugers clattered out of Munro's house, Johnston's boat was slipping quietly out of the harbour. There was no moon and within a minute they were lost in the darkness. From an alley off the harbour square, Munro and his wife Aileen watched the gaugers arrive. It was time for them to head home, back the way they had come.

Grahame's men spent several fruitless hours searching every boat in the harbour. They were watched by almost the entire population of the town, all of whom knew the object of the search was well on its way across to Moray. After a while they were joined by John Munro himself. Seeing the smuggler standing in the crowd, smiling, Grahame realised he had been outwitted. There was no point in calling Munro to court. The man would make a laughing stock of him and the entire Revenue Service. There was nothing to do but admit defeat.

The gaugers lodged for what little remained of the night in a shoreside inn and at first light they clambered aboard the Buckie fishing boat and set sail for Inverness. Not long after they had reached the Highland capital, Willie Johnston's boat returned with the proceeds of John Dearg's latest, profitable venture.

As for Tyler, he was delighted with the two bolls of malt that John had agreed to give him. As he finished his sewing that afternoon, John simply bought the malt back from him at the current rate. He had never even seen the stuff. The smuggler glowered at him as he handed over the cash, grunting," That's a damned expensive jacket you made me."

"Cheap at twice the price, I am thinking," was the tailor's reply.

For the rest of his life Tam Tyler was often heard to remark,

"Being dead sure beats tailoring. I was dead five minutes and made as much as in a month with my needle and thread."

In The Wilds Of Wester Ross

Along the sheltered sea-lochs of the wild north-western coast of Ross-shire the people have always been particularly self-reliant and independent. Regularly drenched by western gales and living between the wild sea and the soaring mountains the their lifestyle was always harsh and demanding. It is no wonder than that these individualistic sons and daughters of the Gael and the Viking had a particular knack for making their own whisky, in defiance of the goverment so far away in London.

In the peatreek years there were gaugers based at Gairloch in Wester Ross and they had an even harder task than their fellows in other parts of Scotland. Apart from the tight-knit communities that banded together to thwart them and the skill and ingenuity of the smugglers, they had the extra difficulty of long distances and rough country to cover in the execution of their duties.

The people around Alligin and Diabaig on Loch Torridon were keen practitioners of the art of the sma' still, and led the gaugers many a merry dance. With the choice of forty miles by road or about fifteen miles through the wild country of Shieldaig Forest around Baosbheinn and Ben Alligin the gaugers never found it easy to catch anyone for smuggling in this area.

The people of Diabaig had a saying *"Is fada Daibaig bho lagh"* (Diabaig is far from the law). With this attitude there is little wonder that stills were sometimes set up in bothies almost in the clachans and villages themselves. There was, at one point in time, a bothy working away happily within a couple of hundred yards of the Alligin schoolhouse. In most cases though, the smugglers did make an effort to keep their activities out of sight. The coastline of Wester Ross is dotted with sea-caves, and many of these were used.

Looking out over the sea to Skye to the north of Diabaig was one such cave that a group of local men adapted for use as a bothy. Led by Donald *Ban* (Fair-haired) McLeod, half-a-dozen men of varying ages had decided to divert a stream running down from the hill of Sithean a Mhill over the cliff above the cave. The waterfall thus created supplied them with a steady supply of water for their activities. As the cave was only accessible from the beach to the south it was a simple matter to send word ahead if gaugers arrived at Alligin. By keeping to the upper levels of the beach which were stony and usually dry the carts left no tracks when they arrived with ingredients and departed with the finished peatreek. The only way the gaugers could discover such a cave was by literally tripping over it. The bothy in the cave was such a success that it carried on for years and was soon copied.

Further up the coast, on the peninsula between Loch Gairloch and Loch Ewe the locals took this idea a stage further. They were much closer to the gaugers at Gairloch and therefore had to be more careful than their cousins at Diabaig and Alligin. It happened like this.

One night in the early years of the nineteenth century a group of smugglers at Melvaig were discussing the building of a new bothy. They were mainly McLeods with a couple of McDonnels amongst them. The month before, one of their stills, which the whole group had worked in a sea-cave south of the village, had been discovered and destroyed by the gaugers. Luckily there had been no-one in the cave at the time, so there was no fear of impending fines, but they had suffered a grievous loss.

Alisdair *Ruadh* (Red) McLeod said, " We will have to be building a new still soon, and these cursed gaugers are wise to the sea-caves."

" We could build one up on the side of Cnoc Breac...," put in Torquil *Og* (Young) McLeod, who was in fact of middle-years.

His friend and contemporary Torquil *Mor* (Big) McLeod broke in, " Och there are already four bothies up there. Another one will be making things a bit too obvious, I am thinking."

There was a general murmur of consent.

" We can be sure that the gaugers will be back soon. " The voice was that of Charlie McDonnell, the oldest man there, who was well into his sixties. He was a man who spoke little, and always to the point. In respect of his years and his wisdom, the others waited for him to go on.

" Now maybe we should give them something to look for," Charlie continued. " A lure if you like."

Everyone was quiet for a few minutes thinking over this idea.

" I have an idea," another voice spoke tentatively. It was Donald *Dubh* (Dark) McLeod, just twenty years old and compared to the others, a bit of a novice at the peatreek.

"Well, young Donald," said Alisdair Ban," speak up. What is this idea of yours?"

" Well," the young man said, looking around the company, " you know the Dark Cave up on the beach near Rudha Reidh....."

" Och, you stupid boy," burst in Torquil Beag. " It is a risk to life even trying to get into that cave. It is of no use at all."

Charlie McDonnell spoke again, " I think Donald Dubh knows that. Am I right Donald?"

" Well yes," the young man replied, his face flushed. He was a bit taken aback by Torquil's attack but he carried on . " I was thinking that if we diverted the stream that's not too far away from it so it made a waterfall into the mouth of the Dark Cave..."

" Now that's brilliant," shouted Alisdair Ban, " brilliant Donald. The gaugers will think that we have a still in the Dark Cave. Oh that will be fun - to see them trying to get into that place. And we can put up the new still in the cave where the old still was. "

There were nods and exclamations of agreement and a few laughs. Donald found himself being patted on the back. His idea appealed to all of the men there. There was nothing they liked better than putting one over on the men of the Excise.

The next few days saw feverish activity as a ditch was dug to the edge of the cliff above the Dark Cave. Once it was finished, the stream was diverted and a brand new waterfall poured its fresh, clear water down the cliff to the mouth of the Dark Cave. No real attempt was made to conceal the new ditch diverting the stream. The sooner the gaugers noticed it the better. Meanwhile a new still was set up in the old cave. Great care was taken to leave the remnants of the old still, which the gaugers had smashed up, lying about the entrance to the cave.

To make sure that the gaugers heard that there was a new still going in the Dark Cave, Donald Dubh and his friend Norman Scambler were sent into Poolewe to spread a few hints. They appeared to get roaring drunk in a couple of the town's inns, so that their apparent carelessness in letting slip about a new still seemed genuine. After all, their indiscretion would probably be put down to the folly of youth, and a touch too much whisky. The two young men dropped several glaring hints, mentioning a virtually inaccessible location and word soon got to the gaugers.

A few days later, a pair of gaugers was spotted with spyglasses on the western slopes of the hill of Maol Breac. They seemed to be very interested in the streams running down to the coastline. They didn't stay very long and once they had gone the locals set back to wait for further developments.

After discussion, the Excise men decided that their best method of approach would be a combined attack along the beach and by sea. This needed more men, so extra gaugers were brought in from Ullapool and Garve. The day of the assault arrived. Early in the morning, half a dozen mounted gaugers set off north from Poolewe through Inverasdale to come down along the beach from the headland of Rudha Reidh. Another six went on board a fishing boat that had been hired for the job and set off to come in from the sea.

As the land group passed up through Inverasdale and round by Loch Sgoud and Loch an Draing, word was sent ahead. The whole peninsula had been warned that there would be a lot of gaugers about, so lookouts had been set. All the still fires in the northern half of the peninsula were doused before the gaugers arrived, which wasn't much of a hindrance, as many of the smugglers preferred to work at night and in the early morning.

Keeping the fishing boat in sight, the gaugers eventually got in position on the beach some way north of the Dark Cave. Luckily the weather was fair and the boat could clearly be seen 150 yards off shore. Signals were exchanged and the two parties moved in. Coming down the beach, the gaugers soon saw the Dark Cave ahead. Smoke was coming from the dark mouth of the cavern. The diverted stream was pouring its waters down the cliff right into the mouth of the cave. The gaugers were exultant- they were going to catch the smugglers red-handed this time, they thought. The problem was that the cave was totally cut off by the sea.

Signalling the boat to sail into the cave, the gaugers sat down on the rocks to see what developed. Meanwhile, out on the fishing boat, things were not going too well. The boat was owned by Willie MacNicol from Poolewe and he did not like the look of the shoreline one bit.

" I do not think I will be able to take the boat in there at all," he said to the local Supervisor, one James Murray. " There are far too many rocks and skerries there. It is too dangerous."

" Call yourself a sailor ?" Murray said sarcastically. " Come on man, just take us in, it's not that difficult.'

" That's easy for you to say," replied MacNicol, " but it is too dangerous I am telling you."

" Maybe you are in league with these damned smugglers," snarled Murray, anxious to have his triumph. " Is that it?"

" I am not," stated MacNicol.

" Well then, prove it," demanded Murray. "Take us in to that cave."

Three times MacNicol took his boat close in and three times he had to pull away. He was an experienced and capable inshore fisherman but there were just too many sharp rocks and swirling, dangerous flows of water to get through to the cave. Even Murray and the gaugers, several of whom were beginning to suffer from seasickness as the boat was tossed up and down, began to realise that they couldn't get into the cave this way.

At last Murray had to admit defeat.

Tales of Whisky and Smuggling

" Take us in to the beach over there where my men are," he ordered MacNicol.

" Will you be wanting me to wait?" asked MacNicol.

"Yes. We will need you to get us back," snapped Murray.

The gaugers were glad to be off the bobbing fishing boat and, wading through the surf to the beach, a couple of them swore to themselves never to set foot on a boat again.

Gathering on the beach, the gaugers listened to their Supervisor.

" We will wait till the tide is fully out. Then we will be able to get in to that cave. It's obvious that the smugglers will have to come out then anyway," he told them. " Till then we will just have to wait."

What Murray and his men didn't know was that the smoke they saw wasn't from a still. Not long before they had arrived, Donald Dubh and Norman had been lowered down on ropes to the cave with bundles of green wood. They had then set a slow, smouldering fire and had been hauled back up again.

Along with quite a few others, they were hiding along the cliff top watching the antics of the gaugers below, antics which were causing a good deal of laughter.

As the day wore on, the weather began to change. Dark clouds started to come in from the west and the wind began to rise. Willie MacNicol was forced to move further out to sea. Squalls of rain began to whip into the beach. On the clifftop the locals headed back to Melvaig. They knew the signs - the weather was going to get worse.

Down on the beach, Murray was getting concerned. The boat was standing further out to sea. Even a landsman like him realised that it wouldn't be able to come back into shore in this weather. All the time visibility was decreasing and his men and he were getting soaked. A further three times he tried to get into the cave as the tide fell. Still they couldn't make it. At last, tired and soaked through he had had enough. By now there was no sign of the boat. As the wind increased and the sea got rougher, MacNicol had decided to run for shelter and was even then beating his way round into the shelter of Loch Ewe.

" We're getting nowhere men," Murray grunted, frustration showing clearly on his broad, florid features. " Let's go. You can all take turns riding back. I'll have that chestnut there."

Choosing the best mount for himself, he led the bedraggled and cold group of gaugers off the beach and south through Melvaig, Erradale and on to Poolewe. By the time they had covered those weary seventeen miles they were soaked through and thoroughly miserable.

Murray was a stubborn man, though, and over the next few months he organised half-a-dozen further attempts to get into the Dark Cave. Whenever they had advance warning, the smugglers would repeat the trick of setting a fire, ensuring that the Supervisor kept trying. And all the time the other stills in the parish continued to produce peatreek unmolested.

On one occasion, the smugglers were almost caught napping. Old Charlie McDonnell and a couple of others were working in a bothy on the slopes of Sithean na Moine, about a mile from Melvaig, when a local boy burst into the bothy to tell them there were gaugers heading down towards them.

"Right," said the old smuggler, " just you get in front of them down by the next burn and when they are quite close, jump up and run straight to Melvaig."

The young lad did as he was told. The four gaugers were spread out looking over the hillside when suddenly they saw a figure leap from the heather and run off.

"There, it's one of their lookouts, after him," the nearest gauger shouted. The gaugers ran off after the boy, finding themselves in the middle of Melvaig a short while later. They followed the young lad into a house in the village, only to find him sitting at a table as his mother cut him a slice of bread.

Looking at the flushed Excisemen she said, " Good afternoon, gentlemen, can I be helping you?"

The four men were too embarrassed to say much and backed out of the humble cottage, mumbling apologies. Back on the hill, the fire was dowsed and the bothy door covered over till the Excisemen were well away.

It was several months before there was a low enough tide for the gaugers to enter the Dark Cave.

None of them ever talked of *that* day. Such was his embarrassment at having expended so much time and effort on such a wild goose chase that Murray never mentioned the matter to his superiors.

Sometimes, however, guile wasn't enough. Loch an Draing at the head of the peninsula was a lonely spot. Only two families lived there and being so isolated they worked their stills in their barns, adjoining the cottages. There was little chance of them being discovered they thought. In fact the peatreek manufacture had carried on undisturbed for such a long time that others came from Inverasdale and other places around the peninsula to take advantage of the peace and quiet. They built their bothies in the surrounding heather.

One day,the gaugers received a tip-off about Loch an Draing from some aggrieved soul and decided to mount a raid. Setting off from Poolewe on

Tales of Whisky and Smuggling

foot early one morning under cover of darkness, they were within a mile or so of Loch an Draing before they were spotted. Word was quickly sent ahead and by the time they arrived at the small group of buildings by the loch, the stills had been removed and hidden. One still had been sunk in the loch, attached to a float by a strong cord, ready to be hauled out again once the gaugers had gone. There was clear evidence of distilling going on in the barns, however - malt was scattered about, and there were paddles for stirring the *browst* as well as several empty ankers.

The five gaugers decided to have a good search of the area and within a few minutes they had located a fifteen-gallon barrel of whisky in a nearby peat-hag or pool, about 200 yards from the cottages. There was no cart anywhere around and the barrel was too big to be carried over the rough track the five miles and more back to Poolewe.

"We'll just have to smash it," said John Malcolm, the senior gauger present. He had just raised a large boulder over his head and was about to smash it down on the whisky-filled barrel when all hell let loose.

Yelling ancient Gaelic war-cries, half-a-dozen men sprang up from the surrounding heather where they had been hiding. At once they grappled with the gaugers. For a few minutes the fight raged. Then Malcolm, felling his assailant, managed to lift his boulder again and smashed the barrel. Out poured the peatreek into the heather. Off ran the smugglers. There was no point in fighting on now. Nursing their bruises the gaugers held a discussion. They had recognised three of the smugglers. They would summons them to court for assault. But there seemed no point in searching on. They had only been there half-an-hour and half-a-dozen smugglers had shown up. They had no idea of how many more there might be close by. So, discretion being the better part of valour, they returned to Poolewe to report their small succcess and swear out complaints for assault against the smugglers they had recognised.

A month or so later, three of the smugglers, all by the name of McLeod, appeared in court and were fined. They asked for time to pay and this was accepted. A week later, a bank cheque arrived, a rare occurence indeed in those days. Even more remarkable, it was signed by the local Justice of the Peace, on whose lands the smugglers had been active! It was little wonder that the gaugers had such a hard time trying to do their job.

Rashiebog

For centuries it has been the practice in Scotland to refer to farmers, whether tenants or owners of their lands, by the name their property. One such was David Ogilvie who died a hundred years ago just short of his own century. Born in 1796 he was actively involved in running a sma' still during, and after, the peatreek years. He lived most of his long life in the wee Angus glen of Glen Quiech, which winds a few short miles into the Grampians between Glen Moy and Glen Ogil. The glen, like so many now, has few occupied houses. All that remains of the substantial farm-toun of Rashiebog are the dykes and a few walls of the steading looking east over the White Burn below. Heather grows over the lands that once grew crops and empty, derelict farmhouses can be seen further up the glen, the last of them having been still occupied into the 1960s. Now the glen is a quiet, solemn sort of place but in Rashiebog's time it had a thriving populace with the "College" at Shallgreen giving education to the many bairns of the glen.

Rashiebog's family took over Hillside farm in the middle years of the eighteenth century and had consistently made their own whisky. Such was his grandfather's skill and love of his craft that he supplied the Laird of Inshewan, his landlord and a relation of the Earl of Airlie with both whisky and ale. In 1785, moving to Horniehaugh, a fine, stone-built house that is still occupied, old Ogilvy had a visit from the gauger based at Forfar, who informed him he must stop this ancient practice forthwith. The Exciseman would have been as well telling the burn to stop running or the birds to stop singing. The only notice the old man took was to move his sma' still into a bothy on the side of Benscravie. Here he carried on making peatreek, instructing his son in the art. In time, the grandson too learned to tend the still.

In his old age, David liked little better than to talk of his smuggling exploits and those of his father and grandfather before him. He himself carried on with the still long after the peak years of the smuggling trade, and there are people who talk yet of finding his still, which was buried somewhere in the glen a few years after his death.

One of Rashiebog's favourite tales concerned his father, also David. It seems the elder David had been discovered one day in his bothy by the Supervisor from Forfar, Mr. Cruickshanks, and a couple of other gaugers. The still and a quantity of whisky were consfiscated and Ogilvy was summonsed to appear at the Black Court in Forfar. By the time he appeared in court, another still was already providing the family and their friends in Glen Quiech with fresh peatreek.

Supervisor Cruickshanks conducted the prosecution himself. On the bench that day was Mr. Proctor, the Factor for Glamis estates and a man who, it may be assumed, liked the odd dram himself.

Having explained the finding of the bothy and the subsequent events the Supervisor went on, " This man is a notorious distiller, an inveterate law-breaker and it is well known that he is a daily trader in illicit whisky. He makes so much of the stuff that it is common knowledge he keeps all the bakers in Kirriemuir in barm (yeast). This scoundrel should be fined no less than twenty pounds".

At this Ogilvy interjected," I have never sold even a gill of barm in my life."

"Mr. Cruickshanks," Proctor interposed drily," is this man appearing here on a charge of selling barm?"

"No Sir, he is not, " Cruickshanks stiffly replied. " He is charged with distilling whisky contrary to the law. As I have said, he should be fined at least twenty pounds to discourage him and others."

Looking at the man in the dock, Proctor asked him directly, "Can you deny distilling whisky?"

" We-ell," our smuggler replied," I cannot do that altogether but it was an awful weary affair I had of it, Sir."

The Supervisor could not contain himself. "The scoundrel admits it. I demand he is punished with the full rigour of the law." he burst in.

" Sit down Mr. Cruickshanks," Proctor said sharply. " I am the judge in this court today, and I will be controlled by none. You are fined three pounds Ogilvy. Pay the clerk. Next case."

Telling this story always made Rashiebog chuckle, " And the judge was right enough," he would say. " There was no sin in making the whisky, and there's was hardly a man in the Braes o' Angus, labourer, farmer, minister or Justice of the Peace, that didn't like a wee drop now and again. If it is all right to make porridge from the oats I grow on my own land then I am sure the good Lord would have no objection to my making whisky from my own barley."

Things did not always work out so well for the smugglers. Like many other devotees of the peatreek, Davie's friend Andra Baxter had little regard for the law. He had a still in nearby Glen Ogil and had been fined on numerous occasions. However, he always returned to the sma' still.

Long after the peatreek industry was declining Andra, like Davie carried on at his old still.

But times were changing and sometime around 1840 Andra was caught by the gaugers again. This time the magistrate was a younger man who had no personal knowledge or experience of the peatreek. All he saw in the dock was a criminal, and an inveterate one at that.

" Do you deny running an illicit still near Haughead in Glenogil Baxter?" demanded the magistrate, a local landowner called Kinmond, initially from England.

" No sir I do not," answered Andra glumly, expecting to be fined.

"Right. We must ensure that the law of the land is obeyed. You are fined two hundred pounds," uttered Kinmond.

Even the gaugers in the court were aghast at this sum. There was no way Andra Baxter would ever be able to pay that amount. It was a small fortune. His friends would never be able to raise such an amount either, so poor Andra had to go to jail, with the prospect of being there for many years. When Davie went to see his old pal in the jail, he expected to find a sad and broken man.

Andra however was full of life. "Just you wait awhile, Davie, and see what happens," he said mysteriously, winking at his friend. No matter how hard Davie pressed Andra, he would say no more.

A week or so later Davie was astounded to see Andra walking up the road to Rashiebog. He ran to greet him.

"What in heaven's name are you doing here?" he asked, clasping him by the hand.

" Ah well, you see I thought that mannie Kinmond was a bit unfair on me. So I wrote a letter," he paused for effect, " to the Prince Regent himself, explaining my case, and," he smiled triumphantly, "here I am. They let me go."

" Now that's a good one, Andra. The Prince Regent. Do you think.....?" Davie let his words tail off.

"Och well, they say he's a man of great taste and refinement, you know," replied his friend with a wink. Laughing together, the two friends went into Davie's house to celebrate Andra's release with a good few glasses of Glenquiech's best.

Whatever the truth of the matter, the two smugglers were convinced that Prince Albert was quite aware of the unique taste and quality of the peatreek, even if he wasn't one of their customers.

Tales of Whisky and Smuggling

Another time about then, Rashiebog was getting ready to light his fire in the bothy on Benscravie with a local lad called Will Menmuir when a loud whistle from down the glen alerted him to the appearance of gaugers. Looking out through the bothy door he saw two mounted gaugers arriving at the school at Shallgreen. The two men dismounted and started up the hill in the direction of the bothy. They were a bit too close for comfort but David was ready for any emergency.

" Right Will," he said," do you see that old sack there?"

"Aye," said Will.

" Well, it is full of old pots and pans that Mrs Ogilvy was throwing out. Now I want you to pick it up quietly and sneak up the side of the burn for a hundred yards or so, being careful to make no noise. Then, when you get to the tree that's fallen over the burn, jump up and run like a hare towards Glen Moy. And let the pots and pans rattle as much as you can. Those government flunkeys will think you have the worm of the still and will chase you. Now take them up the hill and into Moy and right up towards Shank. Do you think you can manage that?"

"Yes, Mr. Ogilvy," said Will, grinning impishly. He had been raised on these hills and knew he could lead the gaugers a merry dance. They would have no hope of catching him in the heather.

Further down the hill, the gaugers had walked over to the burn and were walking slowly up the water's course looking carefully for any sign of a concealed bothy. They were taking their time, knowing they were after a man of great cunning and long experience in the peatreek trade.

Suddenly they heard a clanking noise.

Looking up, they saw a figure dashing through the heather on the hill above them, about seventy yards away. Over his back was a sack that rattled and clanged as he ran.

"He's getting away with the worm," shouted one of them, and both gaugers chased after Will as he took off like a hare. The worm was of course the most complicated and valuable part of the still and with it another still would be relatively easy to set up. So the gaugers pursued the young lad over the shoulder of Benscravie and down into Glenmoy. Every so often, Will would slow down as if winded, but as soon as the gaugers were within about thirty yards he would shoot off again.

The gaugers were young, fit men but by the time they had run the three miles, mainly through heather, up to the farm of Shank in Glenmoy, they were exhausted. Looking back, Will saw first one and then the other come to a full stop and sprawl by the side of the road they had been on for the last mile. Smiling, Will too sat down and had a breather for a minute or two. Then, before the gaugers could react, he was off over the East Burn and disappeared into the woods there.

156

It didn't take the gaugers long to decide to go back to the burn on Benscravie. It was obvious that the bothy was there somewhere. By the time they found it, over two hours had passed since they had dismounted at Shallgreen and the bothy was as clean as a whistle. Rashiebog had simply gone and fetched a couple of ponies and carried his still and his ingredients to another bothy nearby.

" I think what really upset the gaugers that day," Ogilvy would say, " was when they got back to their horses, there was an old sack lying by the tree they had hitched their horses to - the very same sack they had chased all the way up Glenmoy. Their faces were a sight to see when they opened it and found the pots and pans. Ach the poor laddies," he would laugh and shake his head at the memory.

Like his grandfather and his father, Rashiebog took delight in making peatreek and in all his years tending the sma' still he always managed to dodge the gaugers.

" Except the once ," he told a writer from a Dundee newspaper who came to interview him, when he was in his nineties, " when they got an old pot that was virtually useless anyway. Aye, they were great times."

Those times are now long gone, but sometimes, when walking through the all-too-often empty glens of Scotland it is easy to imagine the peatreek stills smoking in their bothies as the people of the Highlands went about their daily lives. Heirs to customs and traditions from time beyond counting, the hard-working, independent Highland people were very fond indeed of their peatreek. It was as if deep in their hearts they all agreed with Robert Burns when he wrote, from experience and understanding, "Whisky and Freedom gang thegither."

The people are gone now from most of the glens but the whole world knows the inspiring taste of the spirit they took so much delight in making and drinking. The quality of the single malts that people of all nations throughout the world can appreciate nowadays is a tribute to those old smugglers who resisted the low quality, factory-manufactured spirits for so long. And next time you "take a dram", drink a toast to the old whisky smugglers, the men and women who tended the peatreek fires..

Epilogue –
How Peatreek Was Made

The main ingredient of the peatreek was barley. Generally 3-4 bolls (180-250Kg) at a time was put into sacks and submerged in water for two or three days. Then it was taken to a barn or similar building where it was spread out on the floor. The next phase was to turn the barley carefully until it had begun to sprout. Then it would be dried, preferably in a kiln, and finally taken to a mill to be ground.

Next the prepared barley was taken to the bothy. Generally built of turf or dug into a hillside, these structures were ususally about 8ft square and built alongside running water. Here, the barley would be put into a vat with a perforated bottom and boiling water would be added. The next step was the "stirring" which was done with a paddle called a "redder". Taking great care at this stage could increase the eventual yield of peatreek by a fair amount. From here, the liquid was passed through a cooler into a large tun, where it was mixed with yeast to induce fermentation.

Once the fermentation was completed the liquid was put into the pot of the still - the *poit dubh* - over a peat fire, and the distilling process itself could begin. The stills were circular, with the top section coming to a point where the pipe which passed the vapour to the "worm" was attached. The worm was a length of coiled copper tubing which was placed in a wooden box, about 4ft high and 3ft wide, called the "flakestand." This receptacle was filled with cold water to condense the vapour in the worm. Keeping the optimum temperature was a matter of skill and experience, with cold water being poured constantly over the worm. The fire too had to be watched closely, as too much heat would cause the spirit to come too fast and be too coarse. The condensed vapour then went from the worm into a pitcher, standing in a tub in case of overflowing.

The liquid was put through this process at least twice. The first spirit coming from this doubling was called 'foreshot' - a lethal combination of

Tales of Whisky and Smuggling

spirits which would be distilled yet again to render it potable. There are sad instances of the young and ignorant dying from having sampled the foreshot. The double distilled spirit was the *Tarraing dubailt* , and being distilled again would become *Treasturring* , or triple distilled. Sometimes the peatreek would be distilled yet again, and this extremely potent liquor was known as *Uisge bea' ba'ol.*

Great care had to be taken at all stages of the process to ensure that the eventual product was of the best. Even the stirring process had people of particular expertise who would go from bothy to bothy hiring out their expertise. A combination of pure, natural ingredients - locally grown barley, burn water and yeast - careful preparation, and the small size of the stills, 40 gallons or less, ensured the peatreek was of prime quality. Other ingredients, including oats and molasses, were sometimes used by those who had less concern for the quality of their spirits.

But just as today the finest whiskies are made from malted barley, so too was the peatreek.

The *draff* or leftover barley was highly prized as cattle food. The leftover liquid was known as *burnt wine* and was poured into the burns. Generally each bothy was worked by two or three people.